Behind Those
Garden Walls
IN HISTORIC SAVANNAH

Text
Louisa Farrand Wood

Paintings
Ray G. Ellis, A.W.S.

Foreword
Thalassa Cruso

Landscape Drawings
Louise Yancey

Horticultural Charts
James White Morton III

Behind Those
Garden Walls
IN HISTORIC SAVANNAH

Historic Savannah Foundation

ISBN: 0-9610106-0-6

First Edition
8000 Softcover
2500 Hardcover

All inquiries concerning the purchase of additional copies may be made to Historic Savannah Foundation, P.O. Box 1983, Savannah, Georgia 31402.

Graphic Design:
Kacey Jones
Frederick Spitzmiller

Coordinator:
Lily Bedford

Design and Printing Consultant:
Douglas M. Eason

4/color Separations by:
Savannah Color Separations
Savannah, GA

Composition by:
RapidoGraphics, Inc.
Tallahassee, FL

Printed and Bound by:
Rose Printing Company, Inc.
Tallahassee, FL

Table of Contents

LOUISA FARRAND WOOD

Louisa Farrand Wood's first creative gardening effort was a highly manicured walled garden in George-town, Washington, D.C. For the next twenty years she lovingly toiled over a wildflower garden on a rocky Connecticut hillside. Thirty-five years later she has come full circle in her gardening career to her most recent but certainly not her final horticul-tural effort, a walled garden in Savannah's Historic District. Through the years, her gardening know-ledge and accumulated wisdom have created many and varied spaces of horticultural beauty.

Mrs. Wood's love of gardening began at an early age and was influenced by a strong family heritage. Her mother, Mrs. Livingston Farrand, designed and created the renowned gardens at the University of Colorado and at Cornell University, when Mrs. Wood's father, Dr. Farrand, was President. Beatrix Farrand, Mrs. Wood's aunt, distinguished for her creation of the famous Dumbarton Oaks garden, was known as the Gertrude Jekyll of America.

Educated abroad, at Miss Madiera's School, and at The New York School of Fine and Applied Design, Mrs. Wood has won numerous garden awards, including The Garden Club of America's Bronze Medal. She is master Découpeuse, having exhibited in numerous museums, and has lectured widely on gardening topics.

For her four years active service overseas during World War II with the American Red Cross, Mrs. Wood was awarded the Army Bronze Star, an honor accorded to few women.

Mrs. Wood is married to William Almon Wood, Professor Emeritus of Columbia University. They have the best of both worlds, for they winter in historic Savannah and summer in Maine. Mrs. Wood relishes the stimulus of her octogenarian years.

RAY G. ELLIS, A.W.S.

Ray Ellis was born in Philadelphia in 1921 and trained at the famous Philadelphia Museum School of Art.

He was elected a member to the New Jersey, Philadelphia and Hudson Valley watercolor socie-ties. In 1964 he was made a member of the presti-gious Salmagundi Club in New York where he later became first vice-president in 1972. In 1969 he was elected to the American Watercolor Society and the Century Association of New York.

Mr. Ellis' first one-man show was at the Pennsylvania Academy of Fine Arts in 1947 followed by shows in various museums throughout the country.

In 1976 he had a one-man show at the Telfair Academy of Arts and Sciences in Savannah and in 1980 established a studio here. This was followed in 1981 by another one-man show at the Scarborugh House.

Acknowledgements

The question has been raised as to why this book has been produced by "new" Savannahians. Possibly the answer lies in the fact that newcomers from all over the world are making their home in this fascinating city, and they look with fresh eyes at the charm and beauty that lies around them, while those who are "native" have always accepted their heritage as a delightful way of life. Demand for "something about gardens" has been another compelling reason for writing it.

When I first envisaged this work, little did I realize the temerity it would take to produce all its components, but thanks to the positive attitude of everyone—well, almost everyone—it took shape.

However, this volume could never have been accomplished without the wise counsel, constructive criticism, and excellent ideas of many Savannahians, both native and new. My indebtedness to them is great.

My gratitude to Thalassa Cruso for her insight and approval knows no bounds.

The distinctive quality of the talented Louise Yancey's landscape renderings has added immeasurably to the usefulness of this book.

The scholarly input of Jim Morton's erudition creates another dimension for those questing further horticultural information.

Organizing the efforts of creative people—including the author and illustrator—would try the soul of any coordinator, but Lily Bedford has risen above it all to help bring our work to completion.

Encouragement has come to me from many, beginning with Audrey Platt, who challenged me to attempt this project; John Hayes, who followed through and urged me onward; Jack Allen, President of Historic Savannah Foundation and his board, who gave this whole effort a most extraordinary vote of confidence, and in particular, Ann Tatum; and the hard working staff, Kacey Jones, Patricia Lord and Rick Spitzmiller, who cheerfully cooperated in so many ways.

I would like to thank Clermont Lee who generously gave of her plans and knowledge; Malcolm Bell, who lent his experienced wisdom; my cousin, Corliss Knapp Engle, for her contacts and horticultural scholarship; Esther Shaver for her book know-how and enthusiasm; Elton Van Brackle for his practical suggestion regarding book size; Barbara Bennett of the Georgia Historical Society for authenticating facts, and Marty Ross for her discerning editorial eye. I am deeply indebted to Richard E. Weaver, Jr., Horticultural Taxonomist, Arnold Arboretum of Harvard University and Ann Crammond, Director, Atlanta Botanical Gardens for checking the accuracy of the vital botanical information.

And I am grateful to Bob Upson, Wendell Graves, Joseph Hunter—nurserymen—and all my garden friends who taught me, a neophyte at southern gardening, so much as I created my own walled garden.

Last but not least, having a live-in editor has made writing this book much easier, and I am grateful to my husband, William Almon Wood, Professor Emeritus, Graduate School of Journalism, Columbia University, for his expertise and tolerance.

Louisa Farrand Wood

Foreword

Urban gardening, which involves the will and capacity to create a green oasis in the midst of an inhospitable environment, holds a spot very close to my heart. London was my birthplace and where I spent my very early formative years. Many of my first memories are of well-kept, small backyard gardens, where my parents produced extraordinary horticultural effects.

Gardening continued over a sustained period is an occupation that calls for lots of patience, resilience after failure, capacity to plan and tenacity to see a job completed. It also demands a strong back and healthy body. These gardening side effects provide excellent discipline and can become the sign posts that lead to an orderly mind. My childhood was complicated, beset with an unusual number of anxieties. Looking back, I have no doubt that what enabled me to cope was my own passionate interest in the natural world in general and in gardening in particular. Even more important, this interest in gardening was for me a nurturing process that quieted my passions and provided a positive outlet for a restless spirit.

Gardening obviously cannot, indeed should not, totally shut out the rest of the world. Nonetheless, over the centuries, down to the present time, gardens and gardening have brought millions of people tranquility of mind and physical well-being that make it possible to face the present, as well as the future, no matter how unsettling.

There is nothing new in this concept. The healing power of gardens has been understood for an immense period of time. The Bible speaks of the Garden of Eden as a perfect place of total innocent happiness. To be driven from it was to lose almost everything, including peace of mind. Archaeological research, reaching back as far as the early Bronze Age, has shown that garden areas existed deep inside the maze of buildings that formed the great urban complexes of the earliest misty dynasties of the Mid-East, the Far East, the Indian sub-continent and the great civilizations of Central America.

From the written record we also know that the Greeks and Romans cultivated medicinal plants and designed enclosed courtyard gardens as places of retreat and pleasure. The spread of the Moslem world to the West added the concept of the use of moving water for visual and cooling delight. The Dark Ages that followed the fall of the Roman Empire eliminated many aspects of the advanced civilization of the defeated Romans. But part of their gardening tradition remained alive and was carried forward with the emergence of Christianity as a missionary force.

The earliest of the Benedictine monasteries of which we have a recorded plan had a fenced or otherwise enclosed area for medicinal plants, as well as indications of spots where food plants and possibly flowers for decorating the church were raised.

Christianity also provided an early indication of an understanding of the power exerted by even the smallest plot of land on the human psyche. Some 11th century Benedictine monks lived in tiny, isolated cells as hermits, each cell having an equally minute piece of land attached to it. This land was

8

laid out in many different ways to suit the taste and aspirations of the individual monk who designed it.

These small parcels of quiet, personal, enclosed space are another fascinating aspect of the slow, many-sided process that produced the diversity of modern gardens. Associated as they are with the isolated monks and a lonely lifestyle, they also suggest a deep and probably very ancient understanding of the therapeutic value of a garden plot, no matter how minute.

In time, the idea of enclosed garden areas was transferred back to the secular world, and the enclosed pleasure garden of pagan times reappeared.

Gardens need not be large or splendid or specially designed for some specific purpose to do their job, which is to rest and refresh the spirit through contact with the unchanging cycles of the natural world. A garden only needs to be nurtured and cherished to fulfill this function both for the owner and the passerby.

For these reasons I am concerned that the gardening legacy which comes down to us from the most ancient urban past should be preserved as an important heritage in our present difficult world.

Thalassa Cruso.

Historic Savannah's Garden Heritage

Seductive Savannah; how fascinating she is! Cities of great charm seem to evoke the use of the feminine gender, and so it invariably is with Savannah, even as with the ships that ply the waters of the curving river that lies at the foot of this celebrated town.

Once, in a well remembered remark, Lady Astor, the former Nancy Langhorne of Virginia and herself a famous beauty, referred to this historic city as "a lovely lady with a dirty face." Well, this lovely lady has now washed her face, wears flowers in her hair and garlands around her shoulders.

Much has been written and said about the glory of Savannah's flowering squares and their original concept by General James Edward Oglethorpe, founder of the Colony of Georgia. However, the admiring sightseer cannot help but be intrigued by what lies behind the high walls of the city's historic houses. This is a book about those walled gardens. But in order to understand their significance, one must first review a bit of their history.

When visitors arrive to explore the enchantments of Savannah's much-publicized renaissance, they are astonished to discover it is primarily a nineteenth century town. True, Oglethorpe landed in 1733 and laid out the plans for defense that became the beautiful squares so much admired today. Few eighteenth century homes remain, for sadly, two devastating fires and a yellow fever plague almost wiped the city away before 1830. After the second fearful destruction, the first fire ordinance was passed in 1834; others followed until 1853, when a fifth and final one decreed all future buildings must be covered with brick, stucco or other non-combustible material.

Probably Savannah's greatest salvation was the city fathers' decision to surrender to General Sherman rather than undergo the horror of Atlanta's fate near the end of the Civil War. For her beauty survived intact, though to many, the heartache of that defeat still lingers today.

The great era of building took place when cotton was king, between 1820 and 1860. Beautifully designed gardens were a delightful adjunct to living. Outlying plantations flourished and Savannah had few rivals as a port. It is this restored nineteenth century historic city the visitor sees today.

During the late Victorian era and at the beginning of the twentieth century, prosperous families wanting larger houses and more land moved beyond the original perimeter of General Oglethorpe's "tything tracts."

Gradually the historic area deteriorated. Buildings decayed from lack of repair, and ornamental ironwork rusted away. Any semblance of a garden became an overgrown tangle of weeds and trash, for sad to relate, the dreadful disintegration had set in. Soon the pouring of asphalt for gas stations and parking lots began, and the old city's aspect changed. One of the most poignant bits of history is Mrs. Laura Palmer Bell's account of the vanishing gardens of her Savannah childhood, written in 1944 for the Georgia Historical Quarterly.

But the blessing was, the bones of beauty remained; the live oaks thrived in the squares, and the churches stood staunchly in place with congregations returning faithfully for services from outlying areas. The port, which had been the fountainhead of so much civilization since 1733, seldom ceased to hum.

The rescue of the nineteenth century part of Savannah began in 1955 with the efforts of seven determined women* and eventually led to the formation of the Historic Savannah Foundation. The renaissance of this city is now a famous chapter in modern urban history.

Those who come to Savannah expecting to find the moss-covered enchantment of Charleston's colonial gardens or the lovingly tended plots behind white picket fences of early Williamsburg are doomed to disappointment. Historic Savannah's gardens are, with rare exceptions, a twentieth century blend of considerable charm with the nineteenth century buildings to which they are attached. To be sure, a number of them are reinterpretations of the old parterre gardens, but the majority are attractive adjustments to the modern world of hybrid developments, personal expression and no hired gardeners.

The term parterre means flower beds laid out in a geometric, often ornate design. They are usually bordered with scalloped tile, brick or dwarf boxwood. Many present-day gardens follow this concept.

One happy result of Mrs. Bell's nostalgia for the gardens of her youth was her seeking the help of Clermont Lee, a Savannah landscape architect. Miss Lee made measured drawings of the few remaining parterred gardens still in existence and, in four cases, the bones of their original design are visible today.

Most of the houses on the old city lots are built adjacent to each other, and right to the sidewalk's edge. The exceptions sometimes have narrow side spaces overlooked by balconies to the east to catch the welcome breezes. The surrounding walls are often of brick lattice, a charming device to permit the flow of air and shield the owner's horticultural whims from the outsider's gaze. Back porches and balconies are distinctive architectural features.

Behind the houses are open spaces, often with a low building at the far end bordering on the service lane. These were formerly used as quarters for servants or stables for horses. Now they are frequently converted into attractive carriage house residences. The open space may vary, but rarely is the land available for making a garden of more than 30 by 30 feet. It is this very confined space that challenges the modern gardener's imagination and knowledge.

In the twentieth century, when time and help are so scarce, practical consideration must be given to gardening. Modern developments in hybridizing suitable plants have helped produce excellent materials unknown in

---

*Katharine Judkins Clark, Eleanor Adler Dillard, Anna Colquit Hunter, Lucy Barrow McIntire, Dorothy Ripley Roebling, Nola McEvoy Roos, Jane Adair Wright

colonial times, and, it would be foolish not to take advantage of them. Modern travel has influenced and raised the sights of many a gardener and this reveals itself in unique personal touches. In Savannah you will find a garden whose inspiration comes from Rome, another whose owner loves the rampant quality of a subtropical jungle, still another with a bit of England, or a restrained riot of bloom in a highly manicured confine. There is one beautiful example of an old garden, devotedly maintained through all these years, that is true to its mid-nineteenth century origin, strongly reflecting its colonial background.

The restoration of Historic Savannah brings several important names to the fore, but the renaissance of the gardens owes much to the quiet efforts of a few women. They set an example by creating gardens for restored houses, many of which now have other owners who have adapted them to suit their own tastes. Individual garden clubs of the city have loyally and lovingly taken the lead in many public projects. As new areas are restored, proper planting is considered as a matter of course. An interesting consequence of this is the expansion of many of the nearby nurseries. Gardening most certainly is making a significant impact on the beauty of Historic Savannah.

Walled gardens have a long and fascinating history, as Thalassa Cruso writes in her foreword. Today, hidden from the public gaze behind the walls of Historic Savannah's houses, there exist modern "Hortus Conclusus;" small oases of privacy and peace. Surely they must be considered treasured possessions in the midst of the turmoil of the late twentieth century. May the pages of this book inspire others to seek the joy and comfort of creating their own island of tranquility.

Louisa Farrand Wood

Small Nuggets
of Walled Garden Wisdom

This is not intended to be a "How To" manual, but a few words of caution about gardening behind walls might be in order, for one purpose of this book is to encourage urban gardening in other cities.

Due to the almost identical limitations of space, there is bound to be a certain amount of similarity in design, but the possible variations of individual expression are enormous. This is accomplished in a number of ways—using different levels, raised beds, curved lines, wall patterns, ground material, water, evergreen and deciduous shrubs, trees, baskets, garden furnishings and lighting—all these can be planned with symmetry and balance to give aesthetic pleasure. This is what the following pages of garden plans attempt to show.

Probably the first and most necessary ingredient to bring to the planning of a town garden is *self-discipline*. The intoxicating urge to acquire every enticing plant seen in a nursery is hard to control. But unfortunately, walls have no elasticity and there they stand, forbidding the accommodation of one more thing. Far better to become infatuated with a few lovely species and have a mass planting for dramatic display. This need not preclude a succession of bloom if the plan is well thought through. Just remember, a "dib and dab" planting does not create an effective design.

The most important key to a successful walled garden is proper *proportion*. The limitations placed upon the gardener are severe. Only by heeding them can the harmonious whole so desired in a small plot be achieved. In selecting material for a restricted area it is wise to think in terms of dwarf and slow growing species or cultivars.

A regular schedule of *pruning* and *thinning* must be accepted as a way of life. A shrub or tree can frequently outgrow its boundaries. This is particularly true in the South, where there is a nine-month growing period. The important factor is to know the habits of your material so you may tackle the job without damaging future blooming. If cutting back is not sufficient, then have the strength of character to ruthlessly remove the offending member. Lament not, for a happy home can always be found with a gardening friend and in its place you will plant a new joy.

The oft-repeated theory that all *color* in nature is harmonious is a complete canard. This is particularly true within the confinements of a walled garden. Careful consideration of color is an absolute must for a serene and happy effect. A fine horticulturist can ruin an otherwise excellent effort with an excruciating combination. The purchase of a simple color chart from an art store can be of great help. Many garden clubs have wheels of complementary and analogous color scales available for further guidance.

One of the most restful results is an all *green garden*. This is often seen in Savannah, for once the wild blaze of the azaleas' spring glory is over, many gardens settle down to variegated and solid greens of interesting texture. This need never be dull, for green comes in many guises. The contrasting shapes, sizes and values of foliage make a marvelous mosaic.

Ground material can be many things—grass, gravel, tabby (oyster shells set in concrete), wood chips, flagstone, slate and brick. But beware of old porous brick, for while charming in effect it tends to become slimy and slippery in the summer's humidity, which necessitates frequent washings with bleach.

Raised beds along garden walls are a way of increasing the planting area, but remember it means additional watering as they tend to dry out more readily than those having the protection of the cool earth.

Fragrance is a delightful component of a walled garden. It is easy to achieve through the use of sweet smelling plants, vines and trees. The warmth of the confined area wafts the scents upward for a rewarding effect.

The sound of *running water* is a refreshing embellishment to consider and can be brought about without too much waste with the use of a recycling pump.

Carefully placed *lighting* enhances the drama for the evening hours and gives additional security to the enclosed area.

Garden furnishings and *ironwork* can greatly help the axis of a design but the scale must be correct for the proportions of the garden.

Trees become paramount for protection, but remember their great thirst in an urban setting where the water table must always be considered.

Temperature within the confines of walls is of the utmost concern and deserves full attention. The problem depends entirely on location—north, south, east or west exposure. Lucky is the gardener who has the ideal amount of sun and shade. So often the merciless, searing down of the sun yields too much heat, the reflection scorches the plant material and hurts the eyes. Whereas, by the same token, lack of sun can produce dank and moldy areas.

For a succession of bloom, *pot gardening* comes to the rescue. Many a frustrated gardener, having only a minute concrete terrace or a few feet of available planting space, seeks the solace of flowers in containers and hanging baskets. These have the advantage of being able to follow seasonal changes. But the all important factor is an almost parental program of feeding and watering.

These are all simply basic problems that would have to be given consideration in any gardening situation. But they become exaggerated with the restriction of space. They in no way detract from the fundamental pleasure and satisfaction all gardeners derive from the joy of creating a new expression of their own.

L. F. W.

Behind Those
Garden Walls
IN HISTORIC SAVANNAH

What better way to begin this book than to show you the garden of one of the quiet forces behind the restoration of historic Savannah's gardens. She herself lives in a house on one of the city's busiest thoroughfares. Her property is a model for all to admire, as she has encircled her home with planting so expertly designed that each side is a charming entity of its own. But the back garden, overlooked from a porch, is the main feature. In the early spring the slatted wood fence, stained a soft gray-green, is covered with pale pink roses that tumble over the top to the street side. People go out of their way for a glimpse of this lovely sight. The inner garden is bordered with boxwood edging, curving gracefully to accommodate a small pool with a stone fountain—two beguiling little children, pouring from a watering can. At the base of the fountain is a lush planting of violets. The center of the garden is a green lawn, to soothe the eyes from the glare of the summer sun.

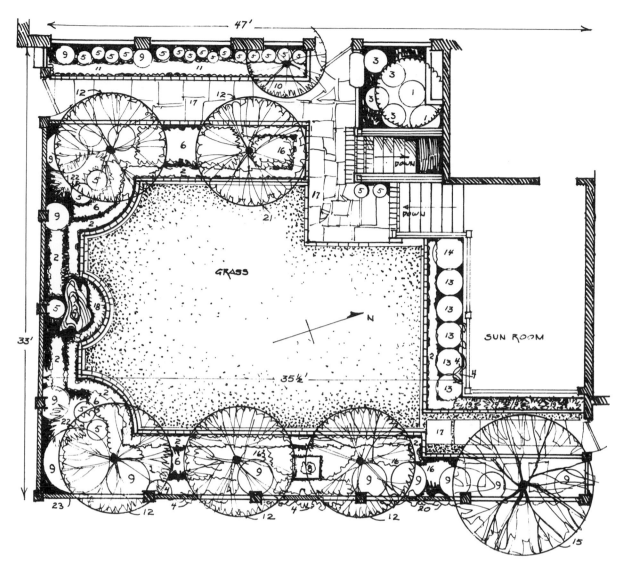

1. Fig
2. Boxwood
3. Rose bush
4. Climbing Rose
5. Pots with various seasonal plants
6. Azalea—dwarf
7. Bronze statuary group in pond—children with watering can
8. Bronze statue—child with bird
9. Camellia
10. Banana Shrub
11. Aucuba
12. Dogwood
13. Raphiolepis Indica
14. Tea Olive in a pot
15. Crabapple
16. Pittosporum
17. Flagstone
18. Violets
19. Ginger lily
20. Jasmine
21. Hanging baskets in tree
22. Holly fern
23. Natural wood, vertically slatted fence

17

A rare remaining eighteenth century cottage is now occupied by one of Savannah's great ladies, whose perfect sense of proportion has created a small jewel of an interior and a little hexagon gem of a garden. She is a very knowledgeable gardener who knows the rules of keeping matters firmly in hand. An offending, overgrown loquat tree was recently replaced with a Camellia sasanqua. A ribbon of ivy runs around the garden's border to accentuate its geometric design. Spring is heralded with pink and white azaleas and a large dogwood tree in bloom. The rest of the year it is a cool, variegated green garden. The focal point is a sculpture by the late renowned Harriet Frishmish. The dancing nymph with a joyous air, and the gaily waving plumes of the Photinia blossoms in the background, make this a happy retreat. On the small front porch, each summer, a potted cerise bougainvillae is the delight of the neighborhood.

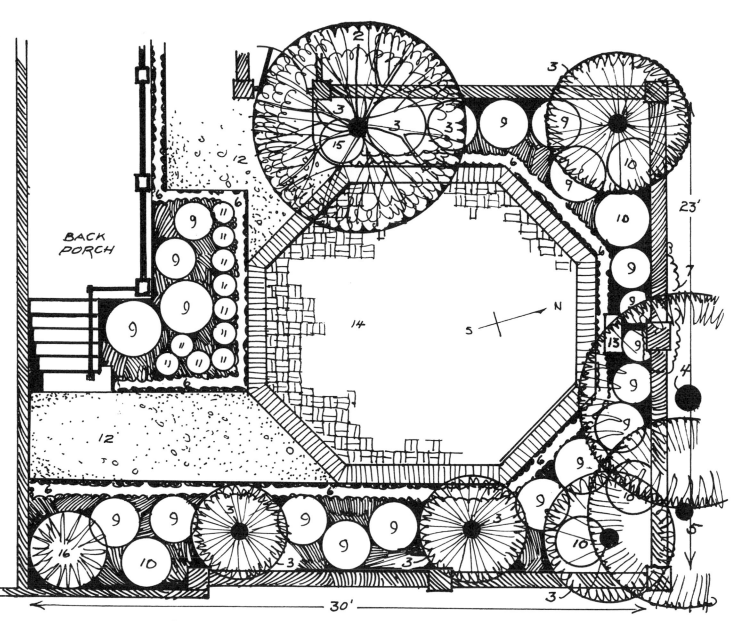

1. Garden furniture
2. Dogwood tree
3. Redtip Photinia
4. Magnolia
5. Tea olive
6. Boxwood
7. Confederate jasmine on wall
8. Trumpet vine
9. Azalea—Karume (pink)
10. Variegated Pittosporum
11. Azalea—Gumpo (white)
12. Tabby paving
13. Statue by Frishmish
14. Brick paving
15. Cleyera
16. Yucca

Probably unbeknownst to the quietly public-spirited owner of this garden, he gives untold pleasure to his neighborhood. As far as a block away, people glancing out of their kitchen windows delight in the constantly changing seasonal bloom of his balcony pot garden. But descending the stairs there is still greater pleasure, for his garden extends the unusual width of two houses. In the spring there is a massed border of bright bulbs. These give way in the summer to gaily colored annuals. A spectacular pyracantha is trained across one wall. Lording over it all is a dignified and ancient crape myrtle tree. Thanks to the double layout, a cool, wide green lawn stretches back to a low carriage house which completes the picture of this mid-nineteenth century garden enclosure.

Grass, while a bore to care for, is certainly the most soothing groundcover during the hot summer months, particularly in a large space. It does not reflect the heat and glare of the sun as much as a paved area.

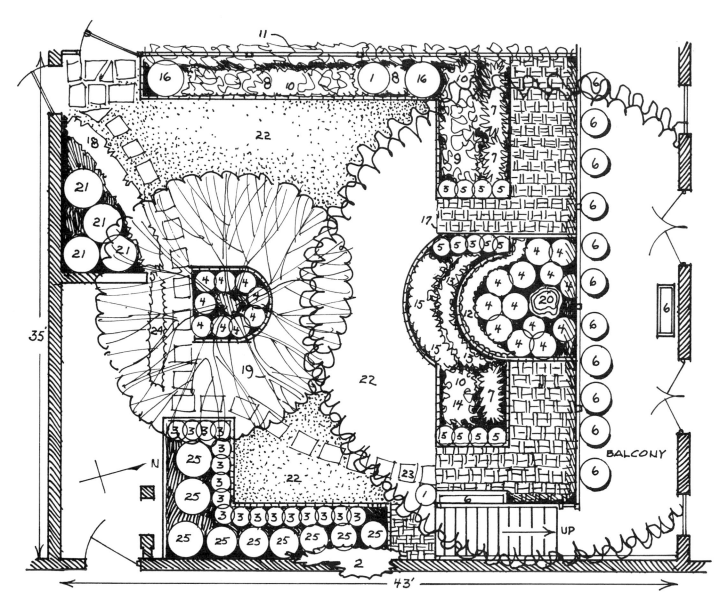

1. Camellia sasanqua
2. Pyracantha espaliered
3. Dwarf azaleas
4. Azaleas
5. Gumpo azaleas
6. Geraniums, impatiens, begonias, taurenia in pots and planters
7. Spider lilies
8. Day lilies
9. Annuals
10. Spring bulbs
11. Confederate jasmine on metal fence
12. Tulbozia violacea
13. Byrd daisies
14. African daisies (gerbera)
15. Chrysanthemums
16. Tea olive
17. Brick paving
18. Yew hedge
19. Large ancient crape myrtle tree
20. Pecan tree
21. Hydrangea
22. Lawn
23. Slate
24. Liriope
25. Camellia

Another of Savannah's great ladies, a pioneer of the Historic Savannah Foundation, confines her gardening to a corner courtyard. Surrounded on two sides by a pierced brick wall, it is dominated by the huge trunk of a hackberry tree. The tree's soft, elephant gray bark makes wonderful harmony with the yellow blossoms of the Parkinsonia tree across the street. In the very early spring, the sweet scent of Daphne odora wafts through the enclosure. Later, pink Raphiolepis comes into bloom, complemented by pink impatiens and pale pink geraniums. On the left street side, a woodbine clambers up the wall, and its brilliant red trumpet heads nod a cheerful greeting to the passerby. Ivy abounds on the opposite wall, in pleasing contrast to the dark red of the wooden front gate. The result is an extraordinarily secluded area for a streetcorner garden, primarily due to the spreading branches of the magnificent tree.

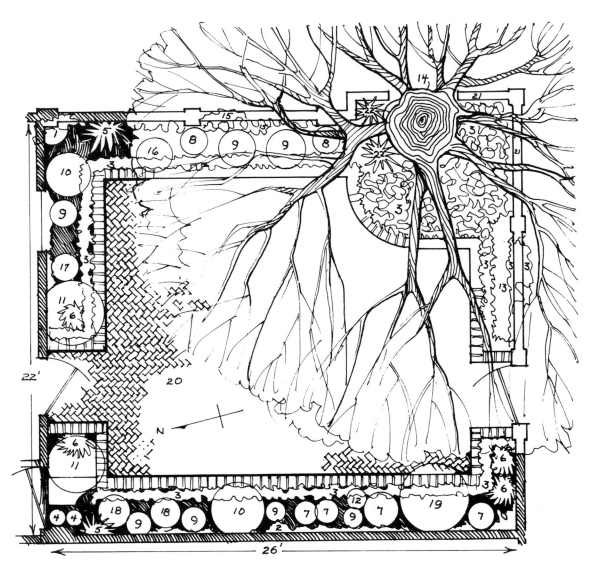

1. Carolina jasmine on wall
2. Fig vine
3. Algerian ivy on wall, in border and under tree
4. Mahonia
5. Yucca gloriosa
6. Holly fern
7. Japanese Boxwood
8. Variegated pittosporum
9. Azalea
10. Podocarpus
11. Cleyera japonica
12. "Iris from the rooftops of China"
13. Leather fern "from the woods"
14. Hackberry/sugarberry tree
15. Coral honeysuckle—woodbine
16. Liquarium
17. Raphiolepis—Indian hawthorn
18. Dwarf pittosporum
19. Viburnum
20. Brickwork—Savannah grey brick
21. Lattice brick wall
22. Yucca aloifolia

An undeniable feeling of Rome is evoked as one steps into this unique sunken patio. Could it be a corner outside of the Borghese Palace? No, it is in the very heart of Historic Savannah. The original owner, who created it in 1964, excavated the ground down to a depth of three feet. The back wall was then built up in two levels, thereby increasing the growing area and giving the illusion of a far greater space than its actual fifteen by nineteen feet. This space is lushly furnished with an extraordinary collection of semi-tropical plants, including palmetto palms that seem to pierce the sky. A chinese Tallow or popcorn tree dominates one side. The small pool with a fountain is centered at the bottom wall. The obelisk and Italian stone figures help to give the feeling that one could be thousands of miles away.

Happily, succeeding owners have appreciated and nurtured this garden, so it remains today a rare retreat hidden in its own special way.

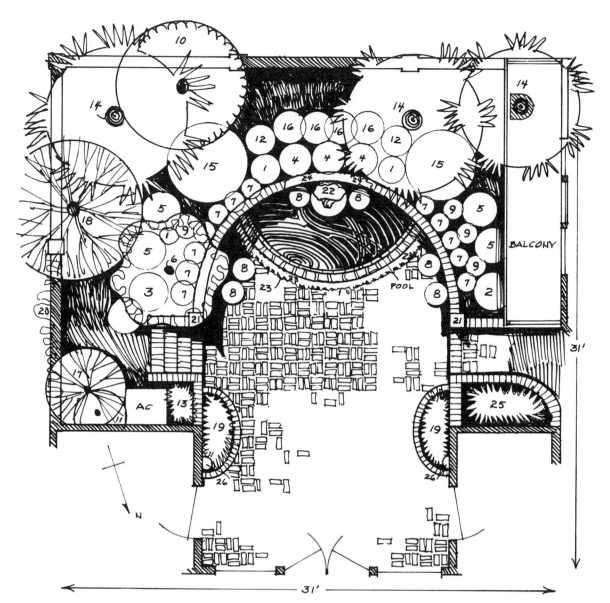

1. Aucula Varigata
2. Azalea Indica—GG. Gerbing (white)
3. Azalea—"President Clay" (red)
4. Azalea Kurume—"Pink Pearl"—dwarf
5. Cleyera japonica
6. Dogwood—Cornus Florida
7. Holly Fern—cyrtomicum Falcatium
8. Pots of house plants, spring and summer
9. Japanese Holly—Ilex vomitoria shillings
10. Magnolia grandiflora
11. Banana shrub
12. Mahonia—beader grape holly
13. Mahonia Fortunei
14. Saw/cabbage palm—Palmetto Sabral
15. Pittosporum Tobria
16. Podocarpus Macio
17. Pear—Pyrus Bradfordi
18. Popcorn tree—Sapium chinese tallow
19. Pittosporum—Wheeleri, dwarf
20. Ivy—tree ivy
21. Stone obelisk 31" high
22. 2 nymphs holding shell on dolphin fountain
23. Asiatic jasmine—trachelospernum asiaticum
24. Fig vine—Ficus repans
25. Hosta
26. Jasmine climbing above doors and windows

Unbelievable as it may seem, all the plant material listed on the opposite page lives happily in this small garden. A distinctive, highly polished band of brass runs along the top of the cast iron balcony railing of the twenty-five-foot-wide house. Attached to the railing, in black iron rings, are pots of bright geraniums. Additional pots march dramatically down the staircase into the much lived-in diminutive courtyard. The brick wall by the side of the steps has a raised bed, giving further dimension to the planting area. At the foot of the back wall a little pool harbors bright goldfish. The dripping fronds of ferns hang from baskets overhead. An iron gate leads to the service lane. On the west side, a small statue stands protected by massed green and white caladiums, while a fig tree spreads over the wall. Under the balcony, a potting shed and garden sick bay are hidden by the palmetto palm tree.

The owner professes not to be a gardener. But the perfect choice and condition of growing things denotes a very discriminating person of taste and great knowledge.

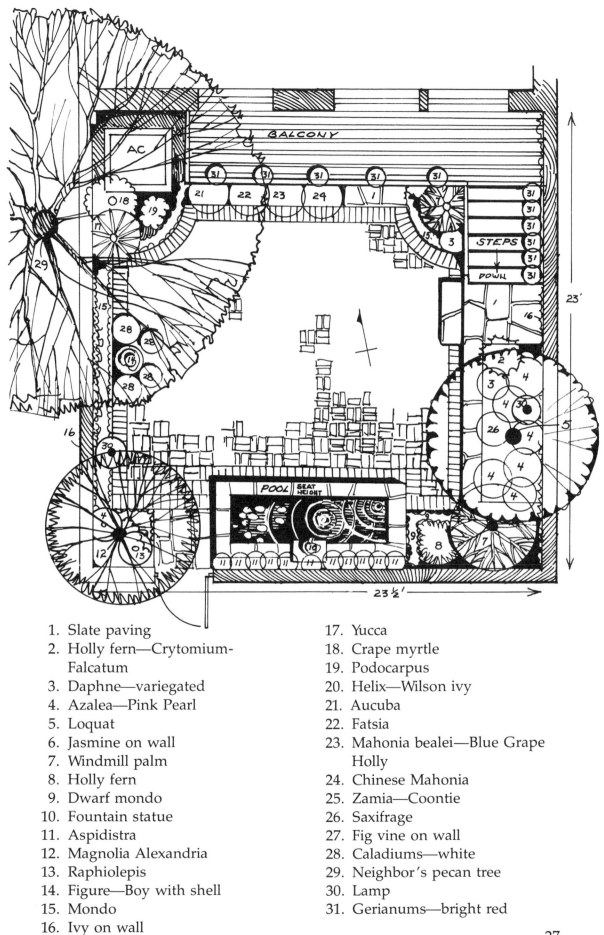

1. Slate paving
2. Holly fern—Crytomium-Falcatum
3. Daphne—variegated
4. Azalea—Pink Pearl
5. Loquat
6. Jasmine on wall
7. Windmill palm
8. Holly fern
9. Dwarf mondo
10. Fountain statue
11. Aspidistra
12. Magnolia Alexandria
13. Raphiolepis
14. Figure—Boy with shell
15. Mondo
16. Ivy on wall
17. Yucca
18. Crape myrtle
19. Podocarpus
20. Helix—Wilson ivy
21. Aucuba
22. Fatsia
23. Mahonia bealei—Blue Grape Holly
24. Chinese Mahonia
25. Zamia—Coontie
26. Saxifrage
27. Fig vine on wall
28. Caladiums—white
29. Neighbor's pecan tree
30. Lamp
31. Gerianums—bright red

27

In spring, when the wisteria is in bloom, one of Savannah's most breathtaking sights is this Italianate Victorian house. It is situated on a particularly beautiful square full of pink azaleas, and the color of the lavender blossoms against the rosy red brick walls, with the yellow Lady Banksia rose and Carolina jasmine on the house next door, make this an unforgettable picture. Walking through the great center hall of the home, a vista of further delight beckons one on: a balcony and veranda dripping with Virginia creeper. Descending the stairs into the deep garden, completely engulfed in semitropical foliage, gives one the feeling of being in the setting of one of Faulkner's novels. The sound of water trickling in the small pool where lilies float, great stands of bamboo, and vines crawling everywhere help to create a truly romantic atmosphere.

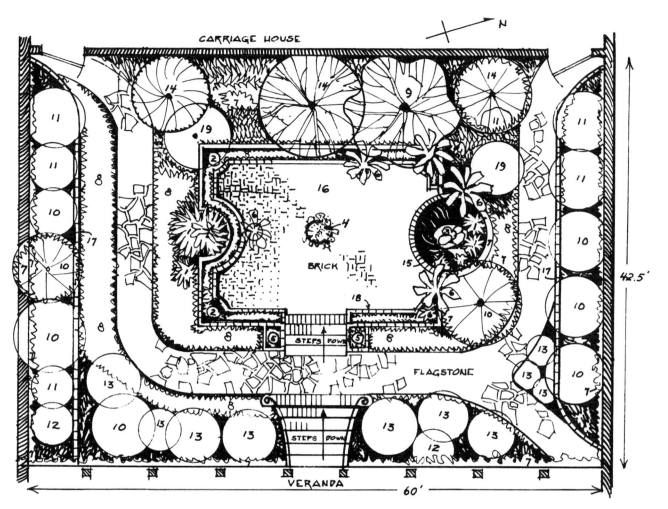

1. Ginger lily
2. Cupid statue—lead
3. Cupid, dolphins with shells—lead
4. Urn on stone pedestal with Asparagus fern
5. Stone ewer
6. Banana shrub
7. Vines—ivy, jasmine, grape
8. Liriope
9. White Maple
10. Crape myrtle
11. Azalea
12. Loquat
13. Boxwood
14. Carolina cherry
15. Pool
16. Sunken area
17. Raised planting beds with brick retaining wall
18. Brick retaining wall
19. Fatsia

The loving care given this little garden reflects the long, honorable career of its owner, a former army nurse. In the spring it is hard to believe such a burst of glory could be contained in so small an area. During that season, slightly below the almost-ground-level back porch, the center brick path leading to the back gate is lined with massed pink and white azaleas. When these subside, colorful annuals follow along the way. On the west wall a great cloud of Confederate jasmine billows out, the white blossoms scenting the air. All this follows the camellias, which have had their turn at bright blooming during the winter months.

Here, everything has its place. A small toolshed at the foot of the garden is a picture of charm and organization. Outside the gate, the hose is meticulously coiled around a clump of Liriope in a manner that would do credit to any military installation.

This is an excellent example of very thoughtful planning, beautifully nurtured material, and disciplined care.

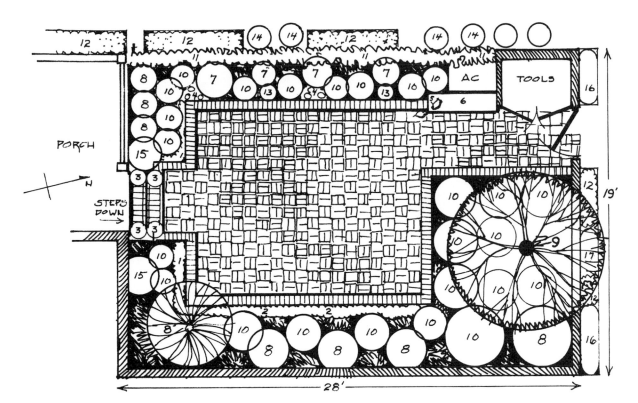

1. Maiden Hair fern
2. Viola odorata
3. Geraniums in pots
4. Small stone figures—elves
5. Bronze birds
6. Stone slab
7. Hydrangeas
8. Camellia
9. Ginkgo Biloba
10. Azalea
11. Japanese Star Jasmine on wall
12. Liriope muscari
13. Begonias
14. Utility Receptacles
15. Holly fern
16. Curly Leaf Ligustrum
17. Variegated Euonymus

This garden is notable for two unusual features—a terrace at each end, and the delicious scent emanating from the tree-sized Tea olive in the center. Stepping out of the back of this home one faces the low carriage house with its own paved area for sitting. Clumps of annuals brighten the picture after the spring awakening of azaleas. Shadows are cast from the lovely tree, but best of all is its sweet aroma. The main house has its own terrace which is reached from the balcony above by a spiral staircase. And the small plot of grass, bordered by shrubs, annuals and herbs, has to be cut with an old-fashioned hand-pushed mower.

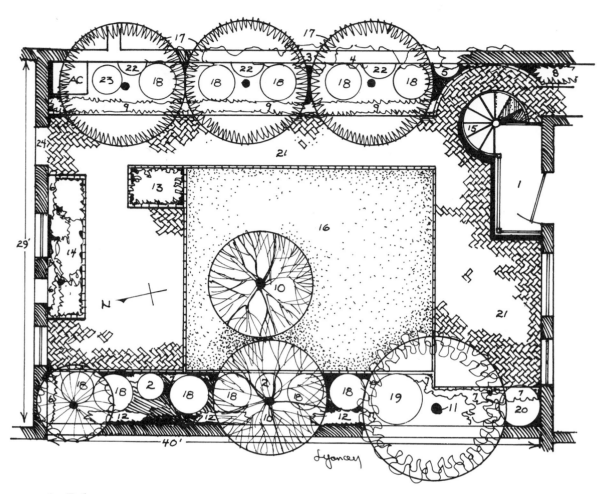

1. Balcony
2. Winter Daphne
3. Ivy on the wall
4. Fig vine on the wall
5. Chinese Star Jasmine
6. Espaliered Pyracantha
7. Ground cover—ajuga
8. Holly fern
9. Liriope border
10. Tea olive tree
11. Carolina cherry tree
12. Pittosporum

13. Annuals
14. Herbs and annuals
15. Spiral stairs
16. Lawn
17. American holly tree
18. Azalea
19. Camellia japonica
20. Viburnum
21. Brick terrace and walks
22. Ardesia crispa
23. Japanese privet
24. Carriage house apartment

A fifteen- by eighteen-foot garden must be called miniature, and so it is with this one which is filled with small blooms and delicate foliage. It is a challenge that could only have been accepted by one of great horticultural knowledge. The owner, widely known in garden circles, has made this an enchanting little enclosure surrounded by high brick walls. A pleasing curve in the retaining wall makes it possible to sit and reach almost any part of the planting area, surely a boon to an active gardener. The tiny balcony, reached by a spiral staircase, extends the flowering space with container plants. The number of species that adhere to this miniscule scale is indeed remarkable. Miniature apricot day lilies, yellow Queen Anne daffodils, blue phlox, rose mallow, blackberry lily, pink evening primrose, tiny pink azaleas and a favorite shocking pink verbena from Sisinghurst Castle in England all live happily in this garden. A large purple morning glory is the only vestige of the original garden built in 1872.

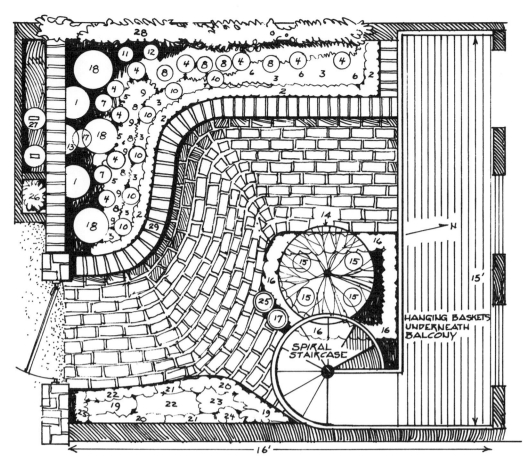

1. Weiger Candida—white
2. Alyssum—white and lavender
3. Verbena (Sissinghurst)—
   shocking pink
4. Salvia—blue
5. Snapdragon—pink
6. Periwinkle—Vinca minor—white
7. Dwarf chrysanthemums—pink
   with yellow center
8. Mullein—"Silver Lace"—tong
   grey
9. Lobelia—blue
10. Ageratum—blue
11. Blackberry lily—yellow
12. Dwarf lantana—lavender
13. Mandavilla—deep pink
14. Dogwood
15. Miniature rose
16. Boxwood
17. Oleander—pink
18. Hydrangea—pink
19. Evening primrose
20. Basil
21. Parsley
22. Rosemary
23. Lavender
24. Portulaca
25. Petunias in pot—yellow
26. Geranium
27. Utility receptacles
28. Morning glory and ivy on the
    walls

This parterre garden has always retained its original plan, and the design is clearly visible today, though Camellia and azalea bushes have grown tall and wide. Of striking beauty in the spring is the luxurious blooming of a lilac bignonia which covers the back wall near the handsome carriage house. Visitors are fascinated by the glass circles that outline the flower beds. They are a traditional use of the bottoms of ordinary stout bottles, imported in quantity from the British Isles in older times.

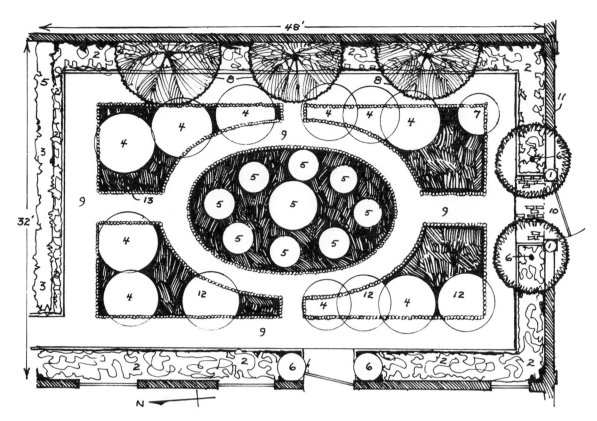

1. Lead finials—century plant in pot
2. Ivy
3. Boxwood
4. Camellia
5. Azalea
6. Podocarpus
7. Cotoneaster
8. Chamaecyparis—false cyprus
9. Brick walkways
10. Ornate iron gate
11. Lattice brick
12. Fragrant Tea olive
13. Edging—stout bottles and violets

One of Savannah's most charming gardens is a riot of pale yellow in the spring when the Lady Banksia rose cascades over the entire back wall. But it is also notable for its side entrance, illustrated above. Behind a beautifully designed black iron gate at the street, the walk leads past utility meters and an air conditioner, a situation common to many city gardens. These are cleverly concealed with large moveable pots of plants that vary with the blooming season. Ivy is carefully trained to assist in hiding these mundane necessities of life. The side entrance door is dramatically focused by two potted plum yew, achieving a splendid architectural effect with their erect form and dark green leaves. A sixteen-inch flower bed at the bottom of the opposite wall is planted with camellias, azaleas and podocarpus. At the far end, the slatted wooden gate is sometimes left open, revealing a slight hint of the delights within. This is an excellent example of how a narrow space can be made horticulturally attractive.

1. Yucca (Spanish Bayonet) in pot placed on aggregated block
2. Begonias in pots—pale pink
3. River pebbles
4. Begonias in pots placed on aggregated blocks—deep pink
5. Camellia—Rubra (red) and Marjorie Magnificent (pink)
6. Aspidistra Lurida
7. Liriope
8. Tree ivy (Fatshedra Lizei) over gate
9. Azalea in pot—Mrs. G.G. Gerbing—white
10. Mahonia in pot—Mahonia Fortunei
11. Podocarpus in pot— Podocarpus Macrophylla
12. Cephalotaxus Harringtonia Fastigata plum yew
13. Aucuba—Gold Dust in pots
14. Ivy and red geraniums in pots
15. Podocarpus
16. Ornate black iron gate to sidewalk
17. Wooden gate to back garden
18. Savannah grey brick
19. Black shutters

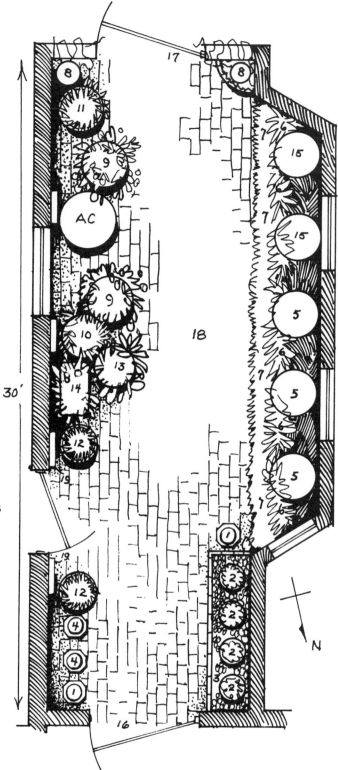

If good bones remain, even a neglected garden can be restored and a new owner can re-establish its charm as a fresh expression of personal taste. In this case, an attractive iron gate in the pierced wall opens into an unusually large brick courtyard protected by an enormous loquat tree. Two levels, achieved by a low dividing brick wall, make the main area perfect for entertaining, an important aspect of Savannah gardens. Pillows placed on the wall become an ideal perch for guests, with plenty of room left in the court for tables and chairs. The main axis of the garden is from the front door of the house looking toward the little pool that burbles happily on the opposite wall. Two viburnum, espaliered on either side of the little figure pouring water from a jug, provide an architectural canopy. The brick wall extends into raised beds which are filled with bloom according to the season. At holiday time two pyracantha, espaliered to resemble Christmas trees, are placed on either side of the front door, the red berries and green leaves making an appropriate greeting to the visitor. In early spring, pink azaleas announce that it is time for outdoor parties again. This garden has been restored by its new owner into a welcoming place of hospitality and fun.

1. Areca Palm in pot
2. Stone nymph with lyre
3. Water plants—iris and water lilies
4. Viburnum odoratissimum
5. Lady Banksia rose
6. Yellow hibiscus in pot
7. Juniperus silvetras in terra cotta pots
8. Azalea—Mary Cochran
9. Espaliered Pyracantha
10. Azalea
11. Abellia
12. Marigolds
13. Curly leaf ivy on the wall—Wilson's ivy
14. Cross vine and fig vine on wall
15. Canna (red)
16. Liriope
17. Mondo grass—Ophiopogon japonicus
18. Pittosporum
19. Loquat
20. Dogwood
21. White spider lily
22. Annuals
23. Pecan tree
24. Podocarpus
25. Mimosa
26. Harland boxwood
27. Awning
28. Grass
29. Brick
30. Viburnum
31. Confederate jasmine
32. Ajuga and impatiens

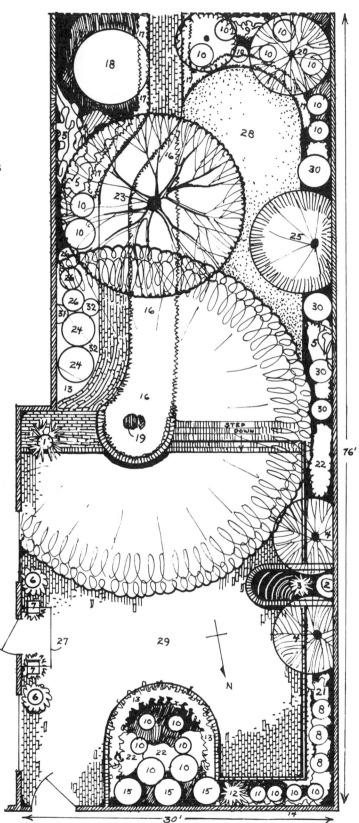

In early January, one of the first glorious announcements of spring is the burst of bright pink bloom on a double flowering apricot tree. This is appropriate because it rises above the walled garden of one of Savannah's acknowledged leaders in the horticultural world as well in historic preservation. Stepping from the house onto the lawn at the same level gives one a feeling of spaciousness. The curving perimeter beds are in constant bloom, for she is, of course, an expert gardener. Even if the interior is not accessible, there is much for the passerby to admire on the outside. Careful planting in the parking area and at the foot of the lattice brick wall always offers something of interest to look at.

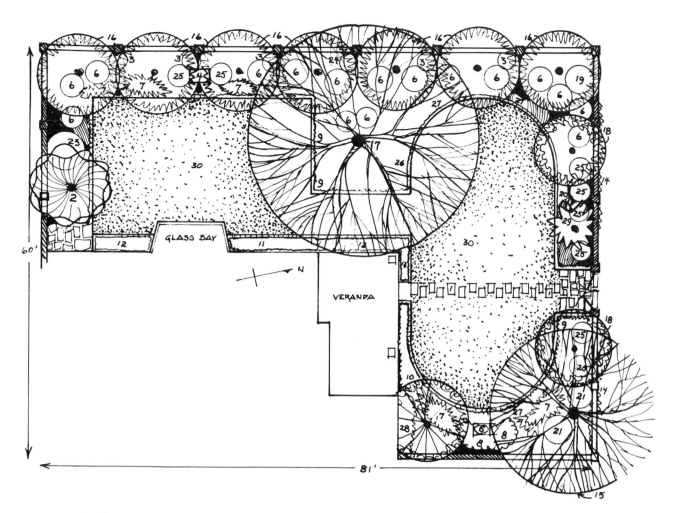

1. Flagstone paving
2. Flowering apricot—pink
3. Camellia
4. Daphne
5. Clam shell birdbath
6. Azalea
7. Holly fern
8. Nandina
9. Ivy
10. Weeping yaupon
11. Dwarf pittosporum
12. Herbs
13. Jasmine asiaticium
14. Jasmine on the wall
15. Live oak
16. Holly tree
17. Paper Mulberry tree
18. Crabapple—pink
19. Hydrangea—blue
20. Annuals
21. Variegated pittosporum
22. Mahonia bealei
23. Sasanqua—White Dove
24. Podocarpus
25. Boxwood
26. Perennial phlox border
27. Bulbs
28. Variegated pittosporum
29. Pine tree
30. Lawn

43

This is a corner of the frontispiece garden. The stone poodles are on guard at the entrance from the street. The owner, looking down from the deck above, designed her garden to be a circle within a square, taking a leaf from the book of William Jay, noted English nineteenth-century architect. Surrounded by terra-cotta stucco walls, it sings with color, carefully orchestrated in tones of shell pink, apricot, salmon, blue, lavender, purple and pale yellow. The beautiful matching terra-cotta brick paths were executed, inch by inch, to perfection by Harry Hunter, one of Savannah's master masons. It is a fall, winter and spring garden. An escutcheon of great sentimental worth from a lamppost at St. Martin in the Field in London is fastened to one wall.

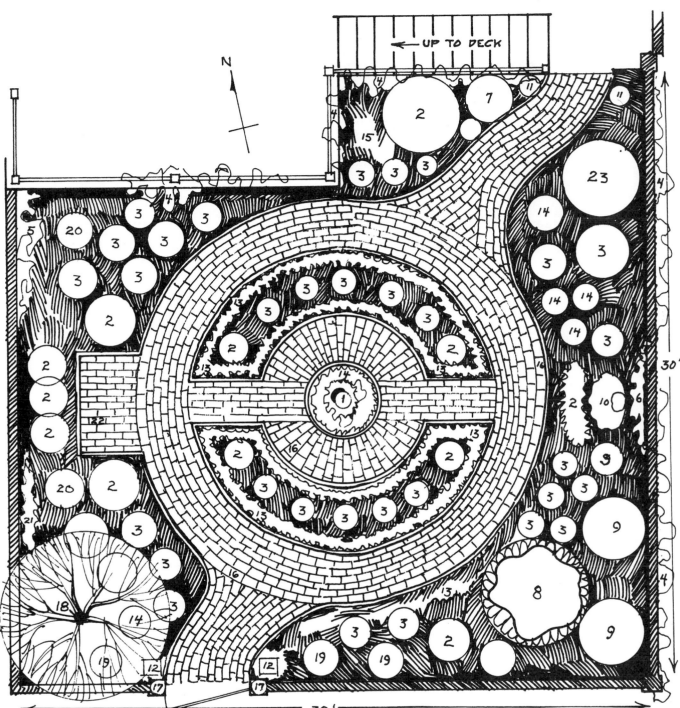

1. Fluted stone pedestal with astral sundial
2. Pittosporum
3. Azalea
4. Jasmine
5. Lady Banksia rose
6. Espaliered pyracantha
7. Nandina
8. Hydrangea
9. Raphiolepis—standard tree
10. Shell birdbath with nymph
11. Stone poodles
12. Terra-cotta pot with yew
13. Ivy
14. Annuals
15. Herbs
16. Terra-cotta colored brick
17. Fruit bowl finials—terra cotta colored
18. Dogwood
19. Juniperus Torulosa
20. Tea olive
21. Espaliered Camellia sasanqua
22. Wrought iron bench
23. Tea olive

A stout heart and a strong back can accomplish near miracles. In two short years, a dirt yard was transformed into one of the most outstanding gardens in historic Savannah. Girding two sides of a large corner house, it is particularly noteworthy in that it has two axes, as seen on the opposite page. It is a delight to walk through a garden where one sees so much of interest. Because the owner is young, enthusiastic and not afraid to experiment, it is full of a variety of plantings. The very fine garden furnishings, as shown in the painting, are unique. On one side of the fountain there is a large, dramatic stand of bamboo. And to top it all off, at the back there is a carriage house with a vine-covered balcony that would make a perfect stage setting.

46

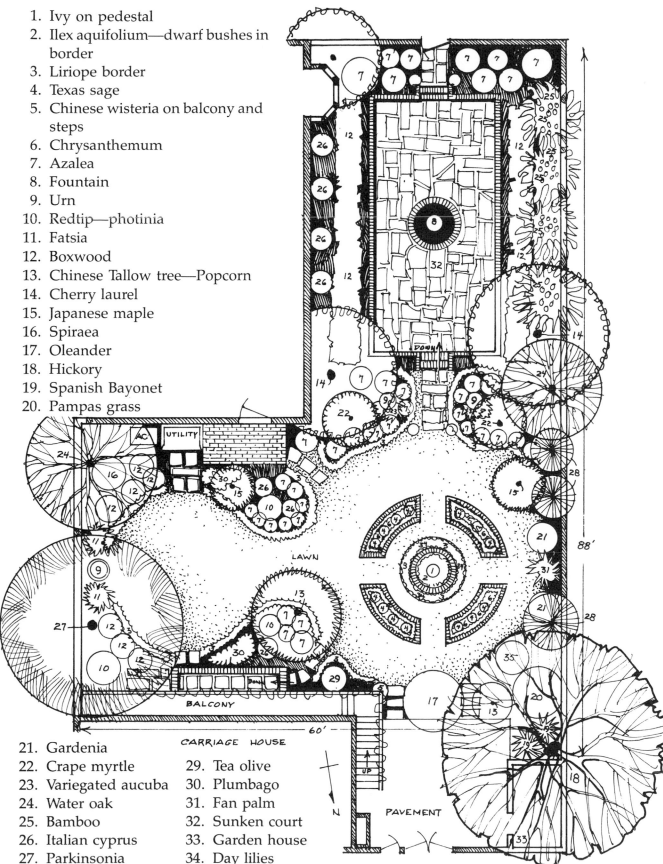

1. Ivy on pedestal
2. Ilex aquifolium—dwarf bushes in border
3. Liriope border
4. Texas sage
5. Chinese wisteria on balcony and steps
6. Chrysanthemum
7. Azalea
8. Fountain
9. Urn
10. Redtip—photinia
11. Fatsia
12. Boxwood
13. Chinese Tallow tree—Popcorn
14. Cherry laurel
15. Japanese maple
16. Spiraea
17. Oleander
18. Hickory
19. Spanish Bayonet
20. Pampas grass

21. Gardenia
22. Crape myrtle
23. Variegated aucuba
24. Water oak
25. Bamboo
26. Italian cyprus
27. Parkinsonia
28. Yellow pine

29. Tea olive
30. Plumbago
31. Fan palm
32. Sunken court
33. Garden house
34. Day lilies
35. Japanese cedar

47

The high stucco walls give no hint of the unusual number of elements in this garden, which wraps around two sides of the house. As you step out the French doors into the main garden area, the little pond is aglow with yellow iris and floating lilies. A border of shrubs follows the contour at the base of the wall. The lawn leads to a small greenhouse, the joy of any gardener. A terrace, shaded by a fine Parkinsonia tree, is at the back of the house. And if you look inside the large glass window you will see a tall Podocarpus flourishing in the atrium. These many facets are keenly appreciated by the present owners, who are gradually restoring the garden to its former peace and quiet beauty.

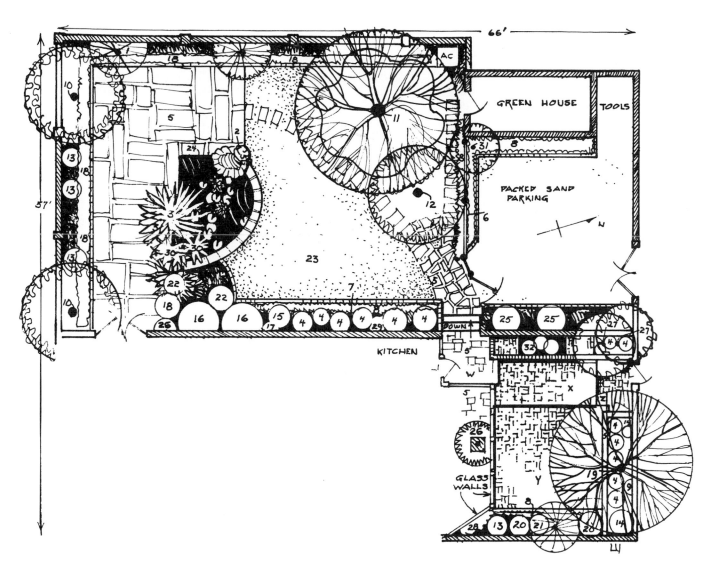

1. Flowering Prunis
2. Statue fountain on a shell
3. Water plants—assorted water lilies, cattails and iris
4. Azalea
5. Slate
6. Confederate jasmine on fence
7. Bushivy—Fatshedera lizei
8. Liriope
9. Cherokee rose climbing into tree
10. Carolina cherry
11. Fig
12. Prunis
13. Hydrangea
14. Pittosporum
15. Pyracantha
16. Ligustrum lucidum
17. Fig vine on wall
18. Boxwood
19. Parkinsonia
20. Flame azalea
21. Holly
22. Holly fern
23. Lawn
24. Pool
25. Purple Leaf plum
26. Podocarpus
27. Yaupon tree
28. Dwarf Buford holly
29. Variegated Pyracantha
30. Umbrella plant
31. Pomegranate
32. Tea rose

As you walk in from the busy street through a gate in the high wall, you are amazed to find so much peace and tranquility in so small an area, only sixteen by twenty feet. The protecting arms of a giant pecan tree spread over a green pocket-handkerchief of a lawn and a ribbon of impatiens is kept to a low border. The round pool with lovely, curving scallops gurgles from the upright jet of a fountain. The small Italian statues of Vincenza stone purchased in Italy many years ago indicate a prescience that foretold, someday, a little corner of restored historic Savannah would be redolent with a serenity that is mindful of a garden in the Old World.

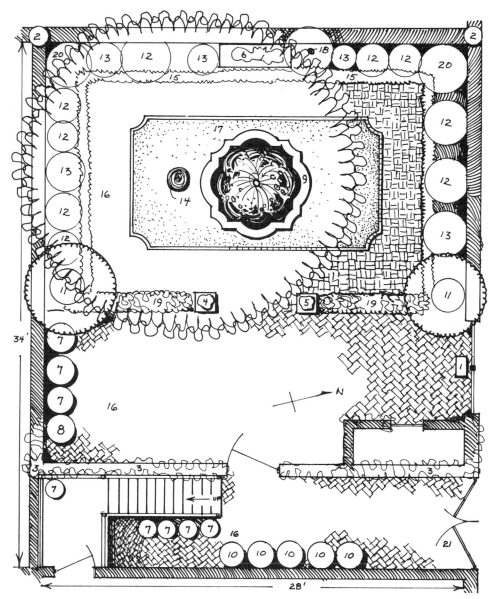

1. Birdbath with cherub
2. Stone urns
3. Fig vine and jasmine on walls
4. Nymph with cymbals
5. Nymph with castanet
6. Fawns with goat
7. Pots with indoor plants (taken indoors for winter)
8. Pittosporum in pot
9. Pool with fountain
10. Yucca in pot
11. Tea olive tree in pot
12. Azalea
13. Camellia
14. Pecan tree
15. Mondo border
16. Brick paving
17. Lawn
18. Carolina cherry
19. Annuals
20. Pittosporum
21. Ornate iron gate

This garden is the pride of Savannah, for it is the oldest town garden in Georgia to survive intact in its original design. Running the length of the veranda and balcony of the Barbados-style house, it is a true parterre garden created in 1852. Always cherished, it is now owned and happily maintained by a descendant of the first possessor. Ceramic tile edges the beds that are bordered with boxwood. Today their centers are being restored with herbs—culinary, ornamental and medicinal. But in the spring this garden is spectacular as it comes truly into its own. The tangled web of Cherokee rose, lilac bignonia, yellow Lady Banksia rose and purple wisteria scrambles up the back wall in glorious disarray. The fruit trees burst into bloom, bulbs push up from the soil, the birds sing and so does all Savannah.

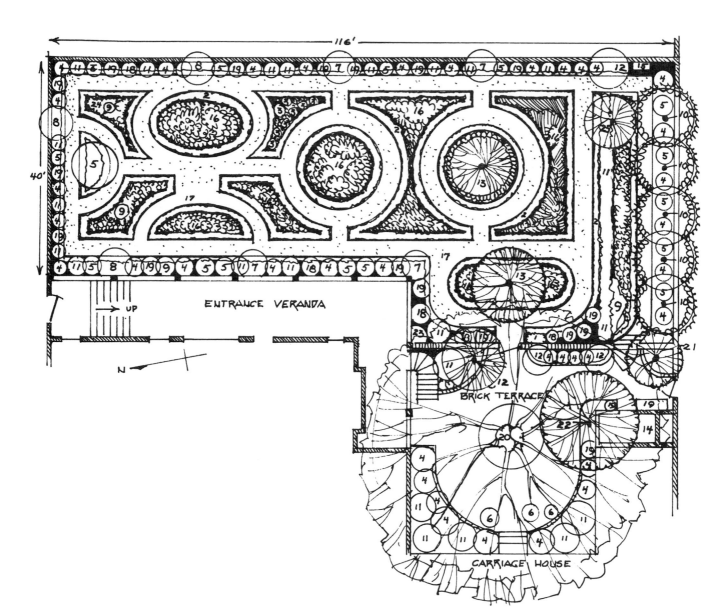

1. Ferns
2. Boxwood borders on all the beds with old ceramic tile edgings
3. Ilex aquifolium
4. Azalea
5. Camellia
6. Pots
7. Podocarpus
8. Loquat
9. Lady Banksia rose
10. American Holly tree
11. Holly
12. Redbud tree
13. Crabapple tree
14. Greenhouse
15. St. Francis in brick niche with iron tracery
16. Annuals
17. Concrete aggregate walks
18. Gloriosa
19. Variegated pittosporum
20. American Plane tree
21. Low wall between front and back gardens
22. Magnolia
23. Jasmine
24. Ajuga
25. Peach tree

One of the largest gardens in Savannah is attached to one of the handsomest houses. The classic pink, brick building dating from 1857 is Italianate in style, but the grounds are pure twentieth century. This could only be a southern garden when the solid bank of pink azaleas bursts into glorious bloom. But once this dramatic display is over, interest centers on the pool, the essence of modern living. Roses climb eight feet up the surrounding white walls, reflecting in the water. The charming architectural detail of the pool house with Confederate jasmine vines weaving up the side pleases the eye. And the comfortable furniture begs one to relax and enjoy the scene. Occasionally the raucous cry of a blue and yellow military macaw rends the air. This neighborhood character—Charlie—is a member of the present owner's family entourage.

The main garden has a simple traditional layout with a center circular reflecting pool. The fountain spills merrily over the bronze statue of a small boy standing on a snail. In the summer, the surrounding azalea beds settle down to a cool green. At that time of year, the pool, a rarity in Downtown Savannah, becomes the hub of activity in this spacious, beautifully maintained walled garden.

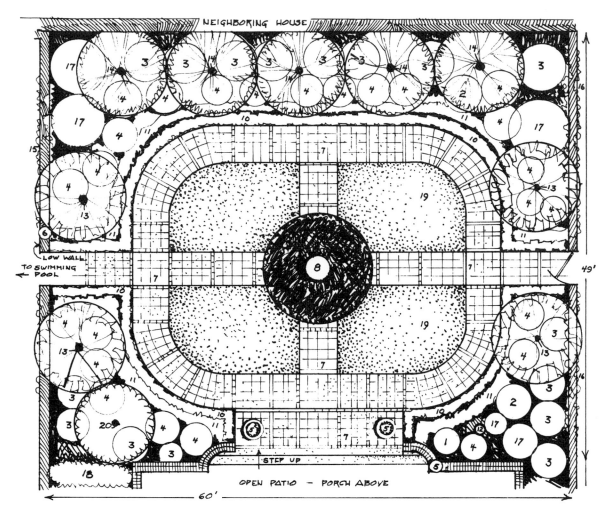

1. Fatsia—fatshedera lizei
2. Hydrangea
3. Azalea
4. Galea
5. Marble urn with geraniums
6. Stone cherub
7. Tabby walk with brick dividers
8. Bronze statue of a child riding a snail
9. Reflecting pool
10. Yew
11. Bulbs
12. Flagpole
13. Dogwood
14. Holly tree
15. Ivy on the wall
16. Carolina jasmine on the wall
17. Camellia japonica
18. Common privet—Ligustrum vulgare
19. Lawn
20. Peach tree

Looking down from the back porch of a beautiful 1797 house, you feel the warmth and charm of the lovely interior pervading the garden too. The present owner, certainly one of Savannah's finest gardeners, generously passes on her knowledge to those who visit on the many occasions that the garden is on tour. In the middle is a small pool completely without mechanism to get out of order. It has a stopper at the bottom for drainage and is simply refilled from a hose when necessary. The goldfish are put in temporary quarters during this procedure. The four beds surrounding the pool are planted with annuals that change with the seasons. The trees and shrubs within the lattice brick walls are kept rigorously pruned to conform to the limited dimensions of the area. This is a garden full of love, from the care given to it by the owner to the many plant "presents" given by her friends.

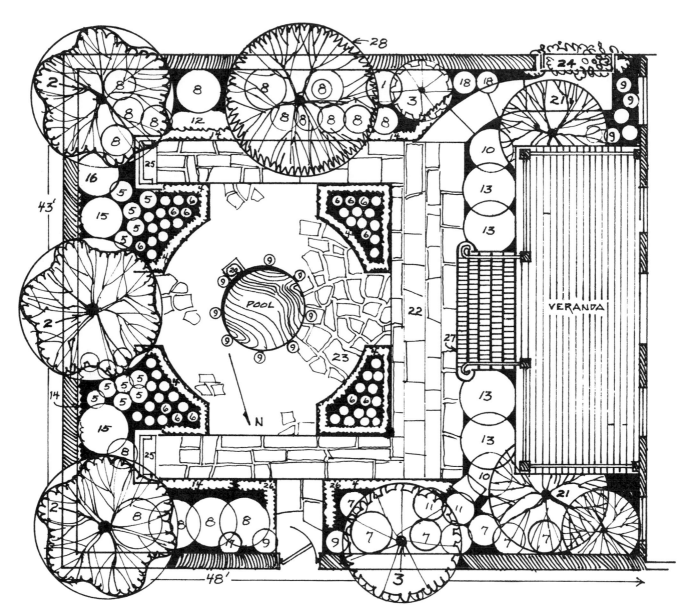

1. Camellia
2. Magnolia
3. Dogwood
4. Trailing variegated euonymus
5. Ligularia—Leopard plant
6. Summer Begonias
7. Azalea—G.G. Gerbing (white)
8. Redtip Photinia
9. Azaleas—Gerbings and
   Waka-bisu
10. Cleyera
11. Espaliered Camellia sasanqua
12. Iris
13. Yew—Podocarpus
14. Ivy

15. Holly fern
16. Hydrangeas
17. Rose
18. Confederate jasmine
19. Pool
20. Cupid statue
21. 'Near East' Crape Myrtle—pink
22. Slate
23. Flagstone
24. Carolina jasmine on arched trellis
25. Wooden bench
26. Blue Rug juniper
27. Steps to porch
28. Carolina cherry

What better fate for a carefully researched, restored garden than to acquire a new owner who cherishes it. An authentic parterre design, it gained fresh vitality with refurbishing and care. Color enlivened the beds with the addition of gerber daisies, bedding plants and, of course, azaleas. The old stone well is the pivotal point where the garden turns to envelop the area back of the house.

No matter how often this property changes hands or what lies in store, the fine bones of the garden design are there, dramatized by the wonderful stand of Crape myrtle, older than the 1854 house itself. No owner could fail to respect so venerable a heritage.

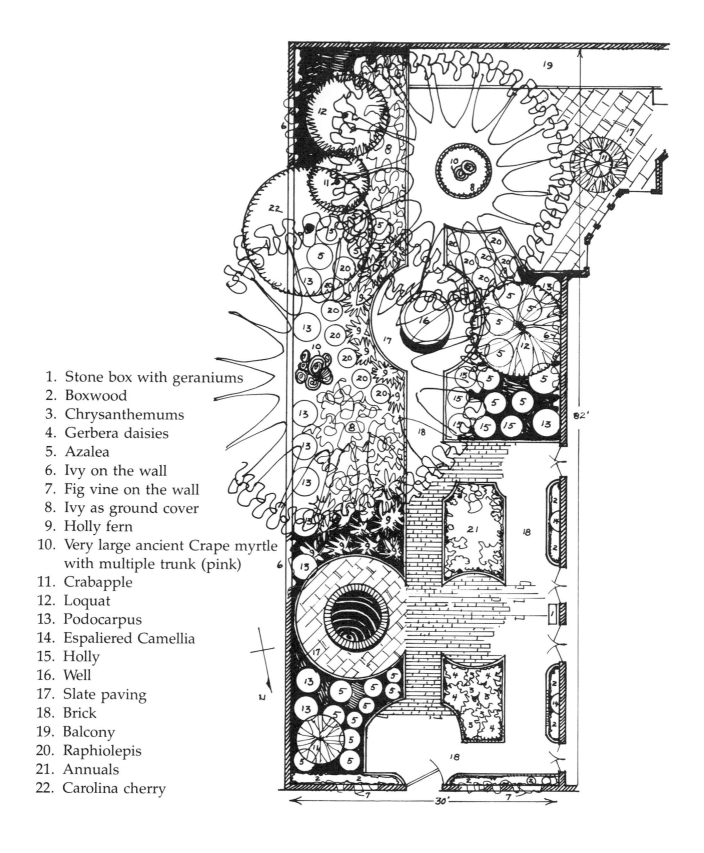

1. Stone box with geraniums
2. Boxwood
3. Chrysanthemums
4. Gerbera daisies
5. Azalea
6. Ivy on the wall
7. Fig vine on the wall
8. Ivy as ground cover
9. Holly fern
10. Very large ancient Crape myrtle
    with multiple trunk (pink)
11. Crabapple
12. Loquat
13. Podocarpus
14. Espaliered Camellia
15. Holly
16. Well
17. Slate paving
18. Brick
19. Balcony
20. Raphiolepis
21. Annuals
22. Carolina cherry

59

A strong gardening heritage can be of enormous assistance in becoming an expert horticulturalist. Such is the case with the owner of this garden. While her layout is simple, it is full of unusual and interesting material. Since this book was started, the tranquility of her plot was shattered one evening when an automobile crashed through the stucco wall, destroying a rare Calloway crabapple tree. Being a stalwart, dedicated gardener, she immediately set about restoring her privacy and planting, but nothing can replace the growing years of that glorious tree. Fortunately such happenings are a rare vicissitude of city gardening.

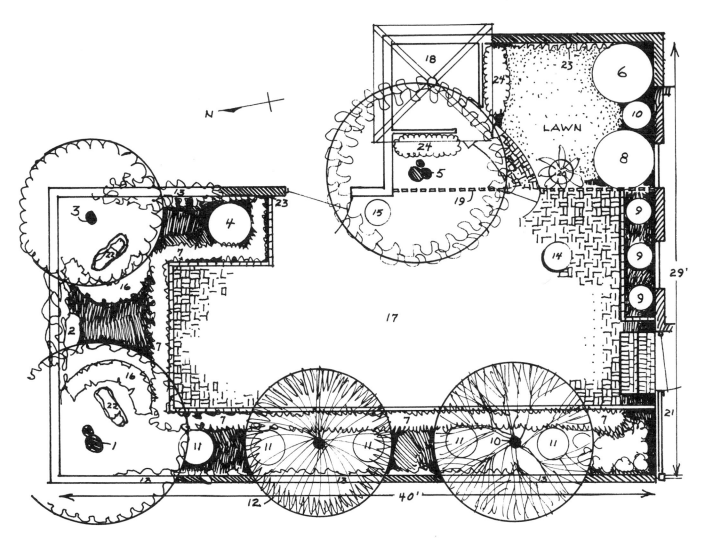

1. Japanese Evergreen oak
2. Lady Banksia rose—yellow
3. Magnolia grandiflora
4. Curly leaf Ligustrum
5. White Crape myrtle
6. Florida anise
7. Trachelospermum (Asian jasmine)
8. Hydrangea
9. Azalea—Satsuki
10. Chinese Tallow tree (Popcorn)
11. Azalea
12. Bradford pear
13. Jasmine on wall and picket fence
14. Juniperus San Jose in terra-cotta pot
15. Sedum in terra cotta strawberry jar
16. Boxwood
17. Brick
18. Tool house
19. Picket fence with jasmine
20. Magnolia Tripetela in pot—Umbrella Leaf Magnolia
21. Screened porch
22. Stone lion
23. Fig vine
24. Pittosporum
25. Lawn

The influence of Savannah's distinguished landscape architect, Clermont H. Lee, is felt throughout the historic area. One of the best examples of her talents lies in the garden of the Girl Scouts of the U.S.A. Headquarters. When its officials purchased the birthplace of Juliette Gordon Low as a means of honoring their founder, they wisely chose Miss Lee to restore the garden, the plans of which had been lost. A period parterre design, circa 1860–1886, was selected, and the drawing on the opposite page clearly shows what a splendid example it is. Terra-cotta tiles border the beds, local gray river gravel surfaces the walks, while the central garden feature—a lead fountain—is surrounded by beds of perennials, bulbs, shrubs and trees. Vines festoon the porch and enclosing walls, which are still surmounted by the original wrought iron fence. This beautifully maintained garden is a credit not only to the Girl Scouts but also to Miss Lee and all of Historic Savannah.

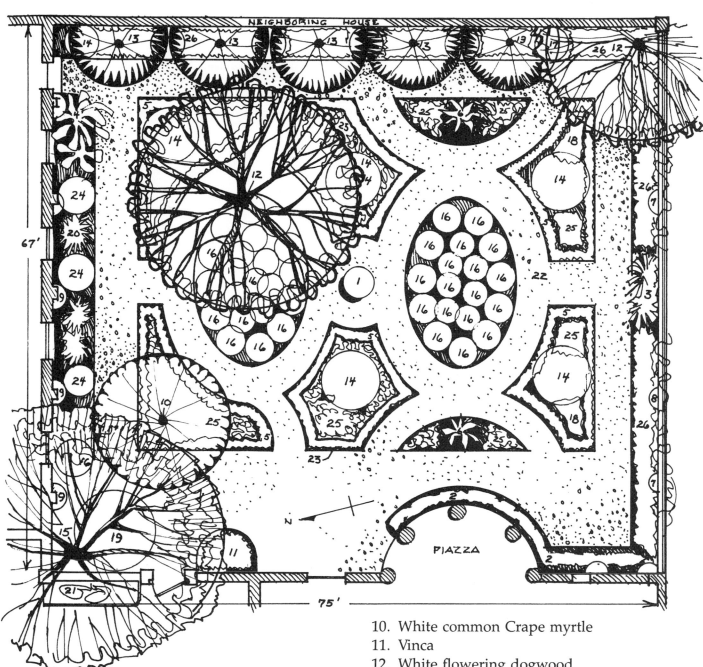

1. Birdbath fountain, swan supported
2. Yew—podocarpus
3. Georgia Easter lily—Lycoris, Red Spider lily
4. Horse banana
5. White Grass Pink
6. Century plant
7. Wisteria on iron fence
8. Jasmine on fence
9. Climbing fig
10. White common Crape myrtle
11. Vinca
12. White flowering dogwood
13. American Holly, var. Savannah
14. Camellia japonica
15. Pecan tree
16. Azalea
17. Hibiscus
18. Iris
19. Tobira Pittosporum
20. Holly fern
21. Bronze cranes
22. Gravel
23. Tile edgings

63

The Owens-Thomas house, probably the most beautiful and best known Regency house in Savannah, is enhanced by the "1820 Georgia style" Regency garden, fashioned in 1954. When one looks down from the back balcony at the parterre design, the eye follows the paths of unusual paving blocks and the mind travels back to England from whence they came. They arrived here as ballast in ships on the return voyage. And one likes to dwell on the fact that General Lafayette also enjoyed this lovely spot while on a brief visit.

The traditional boxwood borders follow the parterre curves, but most of the other plant material is for easy care in today's hurried world. Nevertheless, this recent garden re-interpretation creates an atmosphere that enriches this lovely house.

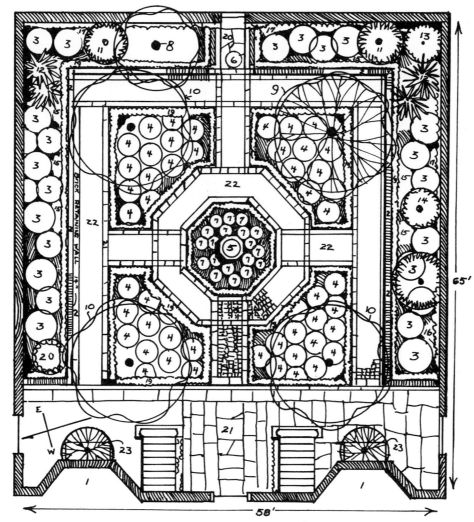

1. Ballast paving blocks
2. Brick retaining wall
3. Azalea
4. White azalea
5. Concrete urn on octagonal pedestal
6. Bust of Caracalla, Roman emperor
7. Azalea
8. Banana shrub
9. Carolina cherry
10. Olive tree
11. Oleander
12. Yucca
13. Crape myrtle
14. Peach tree
15. Day lilies
16. Jasmine on the wall
17. Ivy on the wall
18. Grape arbor
19. Boxwood
20. Grape arbor
21. Flagstone
22. Cobblestone
23. Fig tree

An interesting development in Downtown Savannah has been the conversion of historic properties into delightful inns. With great respect for the heritage of the city, they have been done with care and authenticity. In this particular case, rooms on the west side overlook a neighboring parterre garden. On the east side there is a sunken brick patio with a bubbling fountain. Guests, sitting there for quiet and refreshment, are completely concealed from the sidewalk traffic a few feet away. The proprietor wanted indigenous planting for privacy but also for the edification of visitors. Three Savannah hollies line one wall, and against the other stands a large Photinia. A Tea olive is potted at the foot of the staircase whose railing is wound with Confederate jasmine, and wisteria grows on the balcony overhead. Variegated Pittosporum, sego palm and aspidistra in potted urns fill out this secluded retreat. So successful was the planning by a local horticultural botanist that this garden won a prestigious landscape design award.

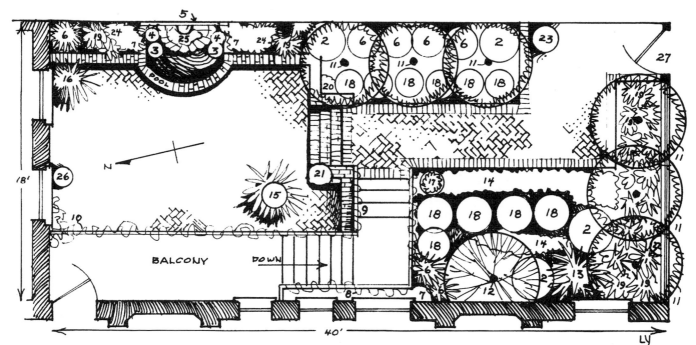

1. Trumpet honeysuckle—Lonicera sempervirens—on fence
2. Pittosporum tobica 'Wheelers'
3. Umbrella plant—cyprus
4. Horsetail—Equisetum
5. Dolphin wall fountain over shell pool
6. Yew—Podocarpus mahi
7. Tree ivy—Fatshedera lizei
8. Muscadine grape on railing—Vitis rotundifolia 'scuppernong'
9. Carolina jasmine—Gelsemium sempervirens
10. Wisteria—Wisteria simensis
11. Savannah holly
12. Photinia fraseri—Fraser Photinia
13. Fan palm
14. Mondo japonica—dwarf
15. Sago palm in pot—Cycas Revoluta
16. Fan palm in pot
17. Tea olive in terra cotta pot
18. Azalea—Waka-bisu
19. Holly fern—cyrtomium falcatua
20. Dwarf nandina
21. Aspidistra in pot
22. Cherokee rose on fence—Rosa lacuigata
23. Variegated pittosporum in pot
24. Flame azalea
25. Ajuga in saucer in the fountain
26. Fig in a pot
27. Iron gate & fence

There is no frustration quite equal to that of the gardener without a garden. However, even the most minute concrete terrace can give some solace with the use of potted plants. While it doesn't offer the same satisfaction as putting one's hands in a little corner of earth, it does give the joy of working with living things. The pleasure of creating attractive pictures of color and variety can be very rewarding. The nurturing process, which is so much a part of gardening, is more essential than ever in pot gardening. Feeding and watering frequently and regularly become duties never to be neglected. Nothing is more depressing than to walk into a pot garden and find it drooping in despair from lack of care.

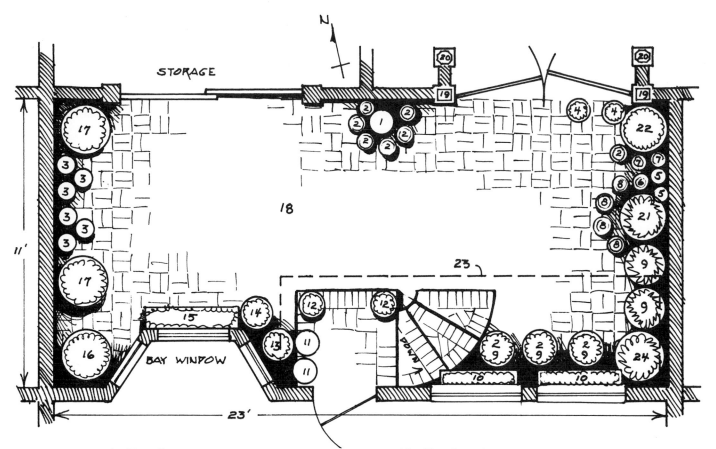

1. Poodle statue
2. Geraniums in pots
3. Ajuga in two wall sconces
4. Hanging baskets of Boston fern
5. Jasmine in pot
6. Begonia in pot
7. Strawberries with ivy in pot
8. Firecracker plants in pot
9. Impatiens in pot
10. Petunias in window boxes
11. Portulaca, jasmine and impatiens in hanging baskets
12. Boxwood tree in decorative urn
13. Daphne in pot
14. Azalea in pot
15. Ivy in box
16. Ficus tree in pot
17. Tree rose in container
18. Brick
19. Truncated obelisk
20. Lantern
21. Hibiscus tree in pot
22. Raphiolepis tree in pot
23. Awning (dotted line)
24. Schefflera tree in pot

Pictured opposite is a small uninspired concrete corner with a stucco wall, made charming by the use of a gray-green Italian scroll holding pots of white impatiens. Beneath it is the bright color of a potted hibiscus. At the base, the sharp note of fire cracker plants is cooled down by potted jasmine at their side. An unusual standard Raphiolepis tree rises up with the curve of the back gate, and a basket of Boston ivy gives a lush furnished look. A glance at the above plan and listing will show you that you can indeed be a gardener in eleven by twenty-three feet of concrete.

Twenty odd years ago this garden was a bare yard outside a stable with a dirt floor. The new owner, with imagination and style, converted the building, in 1960, into one of the most enchanting carriage houses in town. The pink of the curving bay window was repeated in the garden of simple design. Camellias were planted to start in January, big, fat double ones, followed by pink azaleas. The door of the main entrance was dramatized with espaliered podocarpus on either side, while ivy climbed the opposite wall. Beyond the front gate, the sidewalk plot added an attractive note with neatly clipped star jasmine as ground cover.

Though it is an oft repeated truism that gardens usually die with their owners, a glance through the iron gate makes one feel that the spirit of this delightful, witty lady lives on.

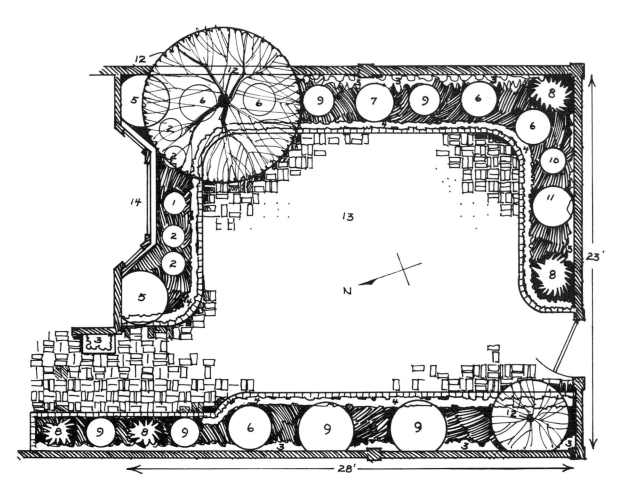

1. Chysanthemum
2. Raphiolepis
3. Ivy on the wall
4. Japanese boxwood border
5. Podocarpus
6. Azalea
7. Nandina—Heavenly Bamboo
8. Holly fern
9. Camellia
10. Daphne odora
11. Loquat
12. Pittosporum
13. Brick
14. Bay window

Other Gardens

The foregoing gardens are a cross-section of what lies "behind those walls" in Historic Savannah. There are other notable restorations that are visible today from the street. As this book grows old, other plans will be drawn up and executed, further enhancing the beauty of this wonderful, old city.

Gardens Open to the Public

Isaiah Davenport House
Green-Meldrim House
Andrew Low House
Independent Presbyterian Church
Trustees' Garden
Scarbrough House (plans drawn)

Garden Owners

Historic Savannah Foundation, Inc. is deeply grateful to the following people for revealing some of the secrets of their walled gardens. From time to time, thanks to their generosity, these gardens are open to the public. Otherwise one must be content with peering through iron gates or peeking through the openings of lattice brick walls.

Mr. and Mrs. Colin Baldwin
Mr. and Mrs. John Brennan
Mrs. John Bouhan
Mrs. John Carswell
Mrs. Reuben Clark
Mr. and Mrs. Peter Coy
Mr. and Mrs. Dan Denny
Dr. and Mrs. Clark Deriso
Mr. and Mrs. Merritt Dixon
Mr. and Mrs. Walter Hartridge
Mr. and Mrs. Mills B. Lane, Jr.
Dr. and Mrs. Lawrence Lee
The Late Mrs. Malcolm Logan
Miss Thelma Matthews
Mr. and Mrs. Ernest Montford
Mr. James Morton
Mr. and Mrs. Dimitri Nicholas
Dr. and Mrs. Harry Portman
Mr. and Mrs. George Ray
Mr. Albert Stoddard
Mr. and Mrs. Hugenin Thomas
Mr. James Williams
Mr. Ben Willingham
Mr. and Mrs. William Wood
Miss Jane Wright
The Juliette Gordon Low Birthplace
The Owens-Thomas House
The Ballastone Inn

Horticultural Sources

Horticultural consensus is difficult to achieve. The following resources have been utilized in an effort to make the foregoing listings as accurate as possible. Some readers no doubt will even dispute these authorities who themselves are not always in agreement.

References

Staff of L. H. Bailey Hortorium, *Hortus Third*. Cornell University, Ithaca, New York: Macmillan Publishing Co., Inc.

The Royal Horticultural Society, *Dictionary of Gardening*. Oxford, England: Clarendon Press

American Joint Committee on Horticultural Nomenclature, *Standardized Plant Names*. Harrisburg, Pa.: J. Horace McFarland Co., 1942

Hudson, Charles J., Jr., *Southern Gardening*. Atlanta: Tupper and Love, 1958

Healey, B. J., *A Gardener's Guide To Plant Names*. New York: Charles Scribner's Sons, 1972

McVaugh, Rogers, *Ferns of Georgia*. Athens: University of Georgia Press, 1951

Perry, Frances, Editor, *Plants and Flowers*. New York: Simon and Schuster, 1974

Seymour, E.L.D., Editor, *The Wise Garden Encyclopedia*. New York: Grosset and Dunlap, 1970

Wigginton, Brooks E., *Trees and Shrubs For the Southeast*. Athens: University of Georgia Press, 1963

Horticultural Nomenclature

From the beginning of time, man has traveled the world and been enchanted by the beauty of exotic flora in strange lands. And man in his travels has always carried seeds and plants as souvenirs of his voyages. The earliest settlers to this country brought seeds from their gardens at home to plant in their new surroundings. Even the slaves from Africa when they first came to coastal Georgia managed to bring in a little handful of the precious benne seed as their secret of health and good luck. Today these seeds are the basis of well-known southern delicacies.

All this horticultural trafficking resulted in much cross-breeding, but also in confusion as to names. At last, in 1753, the distinguished Swedish botanist Linnaeus devised a binomial method of identifying plants—the first name for its genus, the second to designate its species—which has been recognized throughout the world. Although this is the accepted approach to horticulture, there is still a glorious mishmash of nomenclature, partly due to the enthusiasm of amateur gardeners, nurseries, supermarket garden sections and roadside stands.

The following list is an attempt to identify, by both botanical and common name, the two hundred-odd plants that flourish in the 2.2-mile area of Historic Savannah. The seeds of some of these specimens were brought here as part of Savannah's first project, the hope of the new colony, the Trustee's Garden.

Botanical Nomenclature

LISTING OF THE PLANTINGS IN THE WALLED GARDENS OF SAVANNAH

BOTANICAL NAME	COMMON NAME	APPROXIMATE DATE OF ENTRY TO WEST	ORIGIN
Abelia floribunda	Mexican Abelia		Mexico
Acer japonicum	Full-moon Maple	1864	Japan
Acer saccharum	Sugar Maple (white)		Japan & USA
Agave americana	Century plant		Mexico
Ajuga reptans	Carpet Bugle		Europe
Albizia julibrissin	Mimosa: Silk Tree		E. Asia
Alyssum mari timum	Alyssum		Europe
Antirrhinum majus	Snapdragon		Mediterranean
Arctotis stoechadifolia	African Daisy		S. Africa
Ardisia (crispa)	Ardisia		Asia
Arundinaria	Bamboo		Tropics/Subtropics
Asparagus densiflorus 'Sprengeri'	Asparagus Fern	1890	S. Africa
Aspidistra elatior	Cast-iron plant		Japan
Aspidistra lurida	Aspidistra	1822	Asia
Aucuba japonica	Aucuba	1783	Japan
Azalea, see Rhododendron			
Basella alba 'Rubra'	Malabar Spinach		Tropics
Belamcanda chinensis	Blackberry Lily	1823	China & Japan
Begonia coccinea	Angel-wing Begonia		Brazil
Buxus microphylla	Japanese Box		Japan
Buxus sempervirens	Common Box		Europe & W. Asia
Caladium bicolor	Caladium		Tropical S. America
Camellia japonica	Common Camellia	1739	Japan & S. Korea
Camellia sasanqua	Sasanqua Camellia		Japan
Campsis radicans	Trumpet Vine		USA
Canna indica	Red Canna		S.E. USA
Carya glabra	Pignut Hickory		E. USA
Carya illinoinensis	Pecan		E. USA
Cephalotaxus harringtonia 'Fastigata'	Plum Yew		Japan
Cercis canadensis	Eastern Redbud		E. USA
Chaenomeles speciosa	Japanese Quince	1796	Japan
Chamaecyparis lawsoniana	Oregon Cedar		USA
Chamaerops humilis	European Fan Palm	1731	Mediterranean
Chrysanthemum leucanthemum	Ox-eye Daisy		Europe/Asia
Chrysanthemum x morifolium	Chrysanthemum	1789	China
Clethra alnifolia	White Alder; Sweet Pepperbush		E. USA
Coleus blumei	Coleus		Java, or hybrid
Cornus florida	Flowering Dogwood		E. USA
Cortaderia selloana	Pampas Grass	1848	South America
Crinum americanum	Southern Swamp Crinum		S.E. USA
Cupressus sempervirens	Italian Cypress		E. Europe/W. Asia
Cycas revoluta	Sago Palm		S. Japan
Crytomium falcatum	Holly Fern		Asia
Daphne odora	February Daphne		China, Japan
Dianthus plumarius allifloris	White grass pink		Europe, Asia
Endymion hispanicus	Spanish squill		Portugal/Spain
Equisetum	Horsetail		USA

BOTANICAL NAME	COMMON NAME	APPROXIMATE DATE OF ENTRY TO WEST	ORIGIN
Eriobotrya japonica	Loquat		E. Asia
Euonymus japonica	Japanese Euonymus	1804	Japan
X Fatshedera lizei	Tree Ivy		France
Fatsia japonica	Fatsia		Japan
Ficus carica	Common fig		Mediterranean
Ficus pumila	Creeping fig	1721	E. Asia/China
Fortunella margarita	Kumquat		S. China
Galega officinalis	Goats Rue		Europe/Asia
Gardenia jasminoides	Gardenia	1763	China
Geranium maculatum	Wild Geranium		E. USA
Gerbera Jamesoni	Transvaal Daisy		S. Africa
Ginkgo biloba	Ginkgo; Maidenhair		China
Hedera helix	English Ivy		Europe
Hedychium coronarium	Ginger Lily		India
Hibiscus trionum	Flower-of-an-hour		Central Africa
Hosta plantaginea	Hosta; Plantain-lily		China/Japan
Hyacinthus orientalis, var.	Roman Hyacinth		Mediterranean
Hydrangea macrophylla	French Hydrangea		Japan
Hymenocallis caroliniana	Spider Lily		S.E. USA
Ilex Aquifolium	English Holly		Europe
Ilex cassine	Dahoon		S.E. USA
Ilex opaca 'Savannah'	American Holly		USA
Impatiens wallerana	Impatiens; Patient Lucy		E. Africa
Iris germanica	Flag; Bearded Iris		Europe
Justicia brandegeana	Shrimp plant	1936	Mexico
Juniperus horizontalis 'Wiltonii'	Blue Rug Juniper		North America
Juniperus torulosa	Hollywood Juniper		USA
Lagerstroemia indica	Crape Myrtle	1754	China/Korea
Lantana camara	Lantana		Tropical S. America
Lavandula angustifolia	English Lavender		Mediterranean
Leucojum aestivum	Summer Snowflake		Europe
Leucojum vernum	Spring Snowflake		Central Europe
Leucothoe fontanesiana	Leucothe; Dog Hobble		S.E. USA
Ligularia dentata	Ligularia		China/Japan
Ligustrum ovalifolium	Ligustrum; Privet		Japan
Ligustrum vulgare	Common Privet		Europe/N. Africa
Lilium longiflorum var. eximum	Eastern Lily		Japan
Liriope muscari	Liriope; Lily Turf		Japan/China
Lobelia erinus	Edging Lobelia	1782	S. Africa
Lobularia maritima	Sweet Alyssum		Europe
Lonicera japonica	Japanese Honeysuckle	1806	China/Japan
Lonicera sempervirens	Trumpet Honeysuckle		E. USA
Lycoris radiata	Spider Lily		China/Japan
Macfadyena unguis-cati	Catsclaw; Funnelcreeper		Central America
Magnolia grandiflora	Southern Magnolia		S.E. USA
Mahonia aquifolium	Holly Grape		N.W. North America
Mahonia nervosa	Oregon Grape		N.W. USA
Malus pumila	Callaway Garden Crab Apple		USA
Michelia figo	Banana Shrub		China
Mirabilis jalapa	Four O'Clock		Tropical America
Musa x paradisiaca	Banana		Tropics
Nandina domestica	Nandina; Heavenly Bamboo		China/Japan
Nephrolepis exaltata	Sword Fern	1793	Tropics
Nerium oleander	Oleander	1596	Mediterranean region to Japan
Ocium basilicum	Basil		Tropics

BOTANICAL NAME	COMMON NAME	APPROXIMATE DATE OF ENTRY TO WEST	ORIGIN
Oenothera biennis	Evening Primrose		E. USA
Ophiopogon japonicus	Mondo Grass		Japan/Korea
Osmanthus fragrans	Tea Olive	1771	E. Asia/China
Palm Chrysalidacarpus	Areca Palm		USA
Parkinsonia aculeata	Jerusalem Thorn		Tropical America
Parthenocissus quinquefolia	Virginia Creeper		N. America
Philadelphus coronarius	Mock Orange		Europe
Phlox bifida	White Phlox		E. USA
Photinia glabra	Japanese Photinia		Japan
Pimpinella anisum	Anise		Greece to Egypt
Pinus echniata	Shortleaf Pine		S.E. USA
Pittosporum Tobira 'Wheeleri'	Pittosporum Wheelers Dwarf	1804	China/Japan
Plumbago auriculata	Cape Leadwort	1818	S. Africa
Podocarpus macrophyllus	Podocarpus; Japanese Yew		Japan
Portulaca grandiflora	Portulaca; Rose Moss		S. America
Prunus armeniaca	Apricot		China
Prunus caroliniana	Cherry Laurel		S.E. USA
Prunus persica	Peach		China
Punica granatum	Pomegranate		S.E. Europe/S. Asia
Pyracantha coccinea	Pyracantha; Firethorn	1700	Asia Minor
Pyrus calleryana 'Bradford'	Bradford Pear		USA
Quercus acuta	Japanese Evergreen Oak		Japan
Quercus nigra	Water Oak		S.E. USA
Quercus virginiana	Live Oak		S.E. USA
Raphiolepis indica	Indian Hawthorn		S. China
Rhododendron Simsii	Indian Azalea		China
Rhododendron obtusum	Kirishima Azalea		Japan
Rhododendron Gumpo	Gumpo Azalea		Japanese Hybrid
Rhododendron cv.	Ghent Hybrid Azalea		Belgian Hybrid
Rhododendron cv.	Waka-bisu Azalea		Japanese Hybrid
Robinia elliottii	Rose Acacia		S.E. USA
Rosa banksiae	Banksia Rose		China
Rosa laevigata	Cherokee Rose		China
Rosa mutabilis	China Rose		China
Rosa cv.	Houston Tree Rose		USA Hybrid
Rosa cv.	Savannah Tree Rose		USA Hybrid
Rosmarinus officinalis	Rosemary		Mediterranean
Rudbeckia hirta	Black-eyed Susan		USA
Russelia equistiformis	Firecracker Plant		Mexico/Central America
Sabal palmetto	Cabbage Palm		S.E. USA/Mexico
Salvia officinalis	Garden Sage	1730	Mediterranean
Sapium sebiferum	Chinese Tallow Tree		China/Japan
Saxifraga stolonifera	Mother of Thousands; Strawberry Geranium	1815	China/Japan
Smilax lanceolata	Jackson Brier—Smilax		Georgia to Panama
Spirea x bumalda	Spirea		Hybrid
Stokesia laevis	Stokesia; Stokes Aster		S.E. USA
Strelitzia reginae	Bird of Paradise		S. Africa
Tagetes patula	French Marigold		Mexico/Guatemala
Tillandsia usneoides	Spanish Moss		S.E. USA
Torenia fournieri	Torenia; Bluewings		Tropical Asia/Africa
Trachelospermum jasminoides	Star Jasmine		China
Trachelospermum asiaticum	Confederate Jasmine		Japan
Tulbaghia violacea	Society Garlic		S. Africa
Verbascum phlomoides	Mullein	1739	S. Europe

BOTANICAL NAME	COMMON NAME	APPROXIMATE DATE OF ENTRY TO WEST	ORIGIN
Verbena laciniata	Moss Verbena	1818	S. America
Viburnum odoratissimum	Sweet Viburnum	1855	Japan/Formosa
Vinca minor	Periwinkle		Europe
Viola odorata	Sweet Violet		Europe
Vitex agnus-castus	Chaste Tree		E. Europe
Vitis rotundifolia	Muscadine Grape; Scuppernong		N. America
Weigela 'Candida'	Weigela		N. China Hybrid
Yucca gloriosa	Spanish-bayonet		S.E. USA
Zamia floridana	Zamia; Coontie		Florida

Bibliography

A Gardener's Guide to Plant Names, B. J. Healey
Chas. Scribner's Sons, 1972

American Joint Committee on Horticultural Nomenclature
Standardized Plant Names
J. Horace McFarland Co., Harrisburg, 1942

A Nineteenth-Century Garden
Charles Van Ravenswaay
Universe Books, N.Y., 1977

Azaleas
Fred C. Galle
Oxmoor House, Inc.
Birmingham, Ala. 1974

Ferns of Georgia
Rogers McVaugh
Univ. of Georgia Press, 1951

Garden History of Georgia 1733–1933
The Garden Club of Georgia, Inc. 1976

Historic Savannah
Edited by Mary L. Morison
Historic Savannah Foundation, 1979

Medieval English Gardens
Teresa McLean
The Viking Press, 1980

Plants and Flowers
Edited by Frances Perry
Simon & Schuster, 1974

Savannah
>
> Malcolm Bell, Jr.
>
>> Historic Savannah Foundation, 1977

Savannah Now and Then
>
> Cliff Sewell
>
>> The Printcraft Press, Inc., Savannah, 1974

Savannah Revisited
>
> Mills Lane
>
>> The Beehive Press, Savannah, 1969

Sojourn in Savannah
>
> Betty Rauers, Terry Victor, Franklin Traub
>
>> Savannah Visitors Service, Savannah, 1968

Southern Gardening
>
> Charles J. Hudson, Jr.
>
>> Tupper and Love, Atlanta, 1958

The Architecture of Georgia
>
> Frederic, D. Nichols
>
>> The Beehive Press, Savannah, 1976

The Wise Garden Encyclopedia
>
> Edited by E.L.D. Seymour
>
>> Grosset and Dunlap, 1970

Trees and Shrubs For the Southeast
>
> Brooks E. Wigginton
>
>> University of Georgia Press, 1963

Vanishing Gardens of Savannah
>
> Laura Palmer Bell
>
>> Georgia Historical Quarterly, 1944

Authority

THALASSA CRUSO

Known to millions of Americans through her popular television series "Making Things Grow," "Making Things Work," and "Small City Gardens," as well as regular appearances on the Johnny Carson Show, Thalassa Cruso has been guide and mentor to gardeners all across the country. Four garden books, a regular column for the Boston Sunday Globe, the Boston Globe Calendar and McCalls Magazine are part of her immense contribution to gardening. She has won many important horticultural awards, including the Garden Club of America Medal of Merit, the Horticultural Society of New York's Citation for Distinguished Service, and the Garden Club of America's Distinguished Service Medal. Her career includes a scholarly backgrounding in archaeology and anthropology. Born and educated in England, for the last forty-five years as Mrs. Hugh Hencken, she has been an American, but to hear, watch and see her, she is still as English as though she had stepped off the Concorde yesterday afternoon.

LOUISE YANCEY

Louise Yancey, a Virginian widely known as an accomplished water-colorist, oil and acrylic painter, started her education at Hollins College and transferred to Penn State to study mechanical engineering. She obtained a degree at the Washington School of Art and was a member of the prestigious Rangemark Master Class. Later she studied architectural design at Clemson University and studio art at the University of South Carolina where she received her degree in 1977. This background accounts for the distinctive quality of her garden renderings in this book.

Winner of many important awards, she has had solo museum shows and her work hangs in many public and private collections. Now a Savannahian, she and her husband, Bill Streed, own and operate a fascinating architectural antique business called Nostalgia.

JAMES WHITE MORTON III

James White Morton III is a museum consultant who moved to Savannah in 1974. With a Fine Arts Education from the Atlanta College of Art, he soon gained statewide recognition as Exhibits Designer for the Georgia Department of Archives and History (1965–1970) and Curator of the Atlanta Historical Society (1970–1974). He became interested in gardens from the resurgence of horticultural activities on the extensive grounds of "Swan House", headquarters of the Atlanta Historical Society. Jim Morton has done museum design work for such diverse institutions as Martha Berry College, Rome, Ga.; the Madison-Morgan Cultural Center, Madison, Ga.; and the Coastal Georgia Historical Society, St. Simons Island. He is a garden enthusiast who spends his free time working within his own 1850s walled "Messuage" in Downtown Savannah.